PURE SEX

THE INTIMATE GUIDE TO SEXUAL FULFILLMENT

PURE SEX

ANNE HOOPER

PHOTOGRAPHY BY JOHN DAVIS

DUNCAN BAIRD PUBLISHERS

LONDON

Pure Sex
ANNE HOOPER

Distributed in the USA and Canada by
Sterling Publishing Co., Inc.
387 Park Avenue South
New York, NY 10016-8810

This edition first published in the UK and Ireland in 2003 by
Duncan Baird Publishers Ltd
Sixth Floor, Castle House
75–76 Wells Street
London W1T 3QH

ASSOCIATE AUTHOR: KESTA DESMOND

Managing Editor: Judy Barratt
Editors: Joanne Clay with James Hodgson
Managing Designer: Manisha Patel
Designer: Adelle Morris

Library of Congress Cataloging-in-Publication Data is available

ISBN-13: 9-781-84483-330-6   ISBN-10: 1-84483-330-5

10 9 8 7 6 5 4 3 2

Typeset in Gill Sans
Color reproduction by Color & Print Gallery Sdn Bhd, Malaysia
Printed by Imago, Singapore

PUBLISHER'S NOTE: Exercise caution when arranging to meet a person for the first time whom you have encountered via the internet (see pages 120–21) — for example, tell someone where you are going and meet in a public place.

CONTENTS

PREFACE

As a therapist and a writer I've fought to let men and women know that sex is entirely what they make of it, and not what they think anyone else wants it to be. There is no "right way" to do sex. More importantly, there is no right way to think about sex. An individual's sexuality is part of who they are; their sensuality is a share of their spirit and personality and when they are loved, it will be for the unique blend of character that is their own. So, in the purest sense, it does not matter if you swing from a chandelier, or lie quietly with the only partner you have ever valued, it is your very own sexual "essence" that counts.

What, then, is this "essence"? Intangibly, it is a feeling, an impression you give off that represents the inner you – the you that feels adventurous, shy, bold or retiring. If you analyze it with a scientific eye, it is a composite of your upbringing, inherited character, learned information and cultural expectations, all of which build up a unique sexual style.

Can you understand your own sexual style or essence? Can you consciously influence it in any way? The answer to both questions is "yes" and this is the reason why I've written this book. There are many ways we can familiarize ourselves with the workings of that extraordinary sex organ – the brain. Some of them are dotted throughout this book. But understanding sex is a fascinating task, because it isn't just done by thinking – arousing erotic zones of the skin also gets us there. Those erogenous pathways under the surface of the dermis link directly to the brain, sending signals up and down the entire body. And sexual self-knowledge differs from virtually every other psychological discipline in that you can examine yourself emotionally through the gorgeous medium of touch.

You can do this on your own or with a loved partner. You can experience as much or as little sexual pleasure as you desire while doing so. You can be loving and spiritual or lustful and earthy. The essential aim of this book is to help you know your inner sexual nature.

One of the great benefits of the trend for women to buy sex books (a huge social change from 20 years ago) is the way in which this allows subtle influences to creep into the production of such works. When books were designed for men only, they were harsher, cruder and focused on the penis. That is because men, for reasons of biological design, are penis-orientated. This phallocentric view of the world is completely normal. But women, pretty obviously, are not the same.

It is only in recent years that publishing has taken the difference into account. This book, for example, is designed to look gorgeous, to appeal to female sensuality. It is colourful, sensitive, sexy and spiritual. It looks attractive enough to be placed on your coffee table for all the world to see. But it is also practical enough for you to transport it into the bedroom in order to put a few sexual suggestions to the test.

Of course there always have been and still are certain men keen to know themselves through the study of sexuality. The constant interest in Tantric sex shows this to be an ongoing process. But my experience of publishing sex books shows such guys to be rare. Instead, these days men seem to learn through women. When women take books into the bedroom it is both partners who become adept. Logically this means that men in loving relationships are evolving newer, softer ways of being sensual that work alongside the harder, more localized sex response that comes more naturally.

It's not good to be sexist, though, and the experience of lovemaking is no exception. Just as men can learn subtlety and fingertip skills via their women, so too can the women learn from their men. The directness and passion of male desire are intensely arousing. Following the male example teaches women to bypass inhibition and let out the tigers of lust and passion. And if, as suggested on the following pages, you go on to think about your experiences afterward, you will grow increasingly familiar with your own, personal sexual essence – your unique sexual style. It's what this book is all about.

ANNE HOOPER

HOW TO USE THIS BOOK

My aim in writing this book is to help you to explore the world of sex and sensuality and get to know yourself and your body better in the process. To this end, every page contains at least one idea, suggestion or exercise designed to expand your sexual horizons, inspire you or change the way that you think about sex.

I've divided the book into seven chapters. Chapter 1 is called Discovery and it's to help you find out what kind of lover you are. I've devoted several pages to questions about what makes you tick sexually. You can answer these on your own, but if you answer them with your partner you might find they encourage some pretty intimate and revealing discussions. Chapter 2, Seduction, looks at what happens before you get into bed: the flirtation, the romantic rituals – even the food you eat before you make love.

Chapter 3, Sensation, covers all the practical ways in which you can maximize eroticism and sensuality during sex. Chapter 4, Surrender, explores orgasm and how you can make it more powerful by locating your G-spot (that's men *and* women) or by applying ancient techniques derived from yoga or Tantrism. In Chapter 5, Reflection, I encourage you to sit back and just think about your sex life, to observe your sexual rhythms and to talk frankly with your partner about sex. Chapter 6, Exploration, urges you to try all the things in bed that you may have been tempted by or felt curious about. And, finally, in Chapter 7, Troubleshooting, I've written several strategies to help you address problems in your sex life.

Running through these chapters are special double-page spreads, which feature sex positions that I feel have something special to recommend them – either for the man or the woman, or for both partners at once.

Many of the exercises in this book are derived from sex therapy or counselling techniques. I have adapted them for you to use at home with your partner. If, however, you feel that you have sexual or emotional problems that aren't responding to self-help, I would always advise you to seek professional advice from a doctor or appropriate therapist.

We are each unique when it comes to sex. We look for different things in the partners we choose and we have our own idiosyncrasies and peccadillos in bed. Even our belief systems about how men and women should behave sexually are personal to us.

The aim of this chapter is to help you to discover what kind of lover you are, to examine the relationship you are in at the moment and to explore your deeply held beliefs and assumptions about sex. Taking a cool, clear look at your sexual style enables you to move forward in your sex life. You can challenge any attitudes that aren't useful any more and learn to concentrate on simple sensual enjoyment.

DISCOVERY

THE ROMANTIC PATTERN

You believe passionately in the unique bond created by love, and see sex as the ultimate expression of your feelings. However, this most common of approaches doesn't allow for the cooling-off period that all relationships go through. When the initial throes of a new love wear off you may feel cheated of that drug-like high.

LOVE PATTERNS

Self-insight is one of the greatest assets you can have when it comes to sex. Once you understand what type of lover you are, you can work out your strengths and weaknesses and what kind of changes it's possible — and desirable — to make. Although I don't like to pigeon-hole people, we often fall into consistent patterns in relationships and it's useful to be aware of this. See if you recognize yourself in any of these.

THE GAME-PLAYING PATTERN

Game-players tend to treat sex as a recreational activity, and enjoy the thrill of a new conquest or of juggling several partners at once. If you are a game-playing lover you will thrive on short, whirlwind relationships and sexual experimentation, but all this adventurousness can leave you with very little stability in life.

THE FRIENDSHIP PATTERN

Your sexual relationships tend to start out as friendships and develop gradually. They are driven by affection, security and companionship. You value long-term commitment more than the short-term gratification of sexual desire. This pattern can produce wonderful, enduring relationships as long as you don't worry that you have missed out on a grand passion.

THE ALTRUISTIC PATTERN

This is a rare type of love pattern. Sex and passion come low down on your list of priorities in a relationship. Instead you are entirely focused on the needs of your partner and you are prepared to love him or her unconditionally.

THE LEVEL-HEADED PATTERN

If you are a level-headed lover you eschew romance and passion and take a cool-headed approach to relationships, systematically evaluating potential mates before making a commitment. You are likely to make a careful appraisal of someone's background, lifestyle, goals, values and beliefs before deciding that they are right for you.

WHICH ONE ARE YOU?

You may see yourself clearly in just one of these descriptions or you may feel that you display a combination of love patterns. Some people behave differently in different relationships or at different times of life, perhaps following a romantic or turbulent pattern in their youth and then a friendship or level-headed pattern later in life. Consider whether your love pattern brings you fulfilment or whether it creates problems in your love life.

Couples who seek counselling often find that their problems stem from radically different love patterns. For example, the man might be a game-player, while the woman, who has a friendship pattern, is seeking a lifelong companion. Think about your respective approaches to love. If they are incompatible, how far are you prepared to change or compromise? How far is your partner prepared to change or compromise?

THE TURBULENT PATTERN

This pattern of loving is characterized by insecurity. When you are in love you probably find it hard to eat, sleep or concentrate. You suffer from powerful feelings of doubt, anxiety and jealousy in your relationships and this often causes them to self-destruct. You may use sex as a means to reassure yourself of a partner's feelings.

LOVE TRIANGLES

Passion, intimacy and commitment: these are the three critical ingredients in every sexual relationship. Intimacy is that warm, sharing feeling that comes from being emotionally entwined with another person; passion is the sexual spark that gives the relationship its drive; and commitment is the objective decision that, come what may, you are going to stay with your partner.

In 1986, psychologist Robert Sternberg used these three aspects of love to propose his famous triangular theory of love. It's a theory that can be applied to every kind of relationship, and it immediately reveals where the relationship's strengths and weaknesses lie. Sternberg argued that intimacy, passion and commitment combine in relationships to make a "triangle of love". If any of the three ingredients are in short supply or missing, the triangle has mismatched sides or is incomplete.

Of course, in an ideal world, if we all drew our relationship triangles on a piece of paper we would have perfect equilateral shapes in which passion, intimacy and commitment were present in exactly equal amounts. And as love matured the area of that triangle would increase as passion, intimacy and commitment grew and grew.

However, in the real world it's much more likely that one or two ingredients are dominant in a relationship. This doesn't make a relationship unviable, but in such cases it does help to know which areas are lacking so that you can work on them if you so choose. See whether you recognize yourself or your relationship in any of these categories of love.

CONSUMMATE LOVE

This is the ideal type of love in which passion, intimacy and commitment are in perfect balance. If you are in this blissful situation, consider yourself lucky!

INFATUATED LOVE

There is plenty of passion in your relationship but little intimacy and commitment. This might be a relationship that is in its early stages: lots of sex but not much in the way of talking and sharing . . . yet!

EMPTY LOVE

Although you are committed to your partner your relationship lacks intimacy and passion. An example of this kind of love might be a couple who are no longer emotionally or sexually intimate but who have decided to stay together for practical reasons, such as looking after children.

ROMANTIC LOVE

There is lots of intimacy and passion in this type of relationship but not much commitment. Young lovers who may soon be following different paths in life are an example of romantic love.

COMPANIONATE LOVE

You are intimate with your partner and you are committed to a shared future but you score low on passion. This might be a relationship that has endured over many years and in which companionship has taken over where sex left off.

FATUOUS LOVE

Passion and commitment rank highly in your relationship but there is little intimacy. Fatuous love is experienced by couples who don't talk or share their feelings with one another.

LIKING

When you are intimate with someone but you don't have any sense of passion or commitment, your relationship is best described as friendship rather than love. Of course this can change over time – many friends go on to become lovers and long-term partners.

WHICH ONE ARE YOU?

There's nothing inherently right or wrong with any of these types of love. What's important is that the type of relationship that you are in matches your needs and is compatible with what your partner wants. The more you agree with your partner about the emphasis that should be given to passion, intimacy and commitment, the more successful your relationship is likely to be. Discussing with your partner the impact that your love triangles have on your sex life and even plotting your triangles (ideal and actual) on paper can be a fascinating exercise.

WHAT SEX MEANS TO YOU

The statements on the right will help you to think about your sexual style. The first two sections are designed to be completed by you. The final section – sexual aspirations – is intended for you and your partner to complete together, discussing your responses as you go.

There are no right or wrong answers, no scores and no limit to the number of statements you can tick. I simply want you to think about your beliefs and attitudes – and whether they lead you to have fulfilling sex – and, very importantly, to start talking openly and in detail to your partner about sex.

THE ROLE OF SEX

Which of these statements sum up your feelings about the role of sex?

J A ☐ It's a way of expressing my deepest feelings of love and tenderness.

☐ It's the essential physical release whenever I feel turned on.

☐ It helps me to relax at the end of the day.

☐ It keeps our relationship alive and exciting.

J A ☐ It's an ego boost that reassures me that I'm still wanted/needed/loved/desired.

A ☐ It gives me a sense of power/dominance.

J A ☐ It's a way of making up after an argument.

J A ☐ It allows me to express a different side of myself.

☐ Without it I wouldn't feel truly masculine/ feminine.

J ☐ It's a way of becoming intimate again when my partner and I have drifted apart.

☐ It's something I do for my partner's sake/enjoyment.

To discover the roots of your feelings about sex go to pages 92–5.
To find out how to improve your enjoyment of sex go to Chapter 3.

COMMUNICATING ABOUT SEX

Which of these statements best describe your communication style?

- ☐ If I want something in bed I just ask for it.
- ☐ My partner and I have learned over time how to talk about our sexual needs.
- ☐ I'm happy talking about sex but my partner is more reticent.
- ☐ I don't mind talking about sex in general terms but I don't like detailed conversations about who does what.
- ☐ I tend to talk about sex only when there's a problem.
- ☐ I can only talk about sex if my partner takes the lead.
- ☐ Talking about sex takes the magic away.
- ☐ I'm worried that I'd be too critical if I started talking about sex with my partner.
- ☐ I feel dirty if I use sexual slang and a prude if I use medical words.
- ☐ Talking about sex seems corny to me.
- ☐ I find conversations about sex very difficult.

To read about improving sexual communication go to pages 98–9.
To read about discussing sexual problems go to pages 132–3.

SEXUAL ASPIRATIONS

Choose your personal sexual aspirations from this list (or make up your own!).

- ☐ I would love to spend more time on foreplay and an erotic build-up to sex.
- ☐ I would like to experiment with sex toys and games.
- ☐ I would enjoy making love in more adventurous positions and places.
- ☐ I would like to try looking at erotica or enacting sexual fantasies with my partner.
- ☐ I would enjoy more warmth, intimacy and talking in our sex life.
- ☐ I would like sex to include massage and sensuality.
- ☐ I would like to surrender more during sex so I can concentrate on erotic feelings.
- ☐ I would like to have sex more often.
- ☐ I'd prefer to have sex less often and to put more emphasis on quality.
- ☐ I'd like to dominate more during sex.
- ☐ I'd like to play a more passive sexual role.

To read about enhancing intimacy and sensuality go to Chapter 3.
To read about sexual experimentation go to Chapter 6.

SEX FOR HIM

Here we focus on how the male partner views sex. The first column – male sexuality – is for you both to look at together. Find the subjects that you agree and disagree on and discuss why you hold the opinions you do. The other two columns are for men to look at on their own. There are no right or wrong answers, no scores and no limit to the number of statements you can tick. Try to think about how your attitudes and feelings about sex and sexuality impact on your day-to-day enjoyment of sex.

MALE SEXUALITY

Which of these statements best match your feelings about male sexuality?

☐ Men think about sex all the time.

☐ Men are sexual predators.

☐ Men's sexual feelings are based on lust rather than love.

☐ Men prefer to have sex with no strings attached.

☐ Men need to have sex for the physical release it brings.

☐ Men can be hampered sexually because they are taught that it's weak or unmasculine to show their emotions.

☐ Men are socialized to be sexually dominant but this isn't necessarily their true nature.

☐ All men are different and it's difficult to make generalizations.

☐ There is no real difference between male and female sexuality.

To read about pushing back the boundaries during sex go to pages 106–107.
To read about exploding sexual myths go to pages 108–109.

SEXUAL PERFORMANCE

Which of these statements describe your feelings about sexual performance?

- ☐ I'm happy with my sexual performance.
- ☐ There's always room for improvement, but I think I'm OK in bed.
- ☐ I don't feel confident about my ability to arouse my partner.
- ☐ I'm not sure how to bring my partner to orgasm.
- ☐ Sex would be better if I could make it last a bit longer.
- ☐ Sex is disappointing because I always come too quickly.
- ☐ I find it difficult to get/keep an erection.
- ☐ I'd enjoy sex more if I spent less time worrying about my performance.
- ☐ My performance anxieties make it very difficult for me to have any sort of sex with a partner.

To read about how to have long, sensual sex go to pages 36–7.
To read about special sex techniques go to pages 76–9 and 82–7.
To read about solving sex problems go to Chapter 7.

ATTITUDES TOWARD WOMEN

Which of these statements reflect your attitudes to women?

- ☐ I've always got on well with women both in and out of bed.
- ☐ I've had mixed relationships with women; some good, some bad.
- ☐ I have rarely had a non-sexual relationship with a woman.
- ☐ I've got good female friends but my sexual relationships are less successful.
- ☐ I've had problems in all my relationships with women.
- ☐ I find women hard to talk to.
- ☐ I find women too demanding.
- ☐ I feel shy or inhibited whenever I'm around women.
- ☐ Women are only really interested in good-looking men.
- ☐ Women always seem to reject me sexually.

To read about the secrets of attraction and attractiveness go to pages 28–9.
To read about seduction go to Chapter 2.

SEX FOR HER

Here we explore women's attitudes to sex. The first column is for you both to look at, discussing your responses as you go. If you disagree with each other, try to find out why. If you agree, talk about the experiences that have informed your views. The other three columns are for women to go through by themselves. There are no right or wrong answers, no scores and no limit to the number of statements you can tick. Try to think about how your attitudes and self-image affect the way you express yourself sexually.

FEMALE SEXUALITY

Which of these statements best match your feelings about female sexuality?

☐ Women have a gentle and romantic approach to sex.

☐ Women have a lower libido than men.

☐ Women are naturally monogamous.

☐ Women prefer sex in a committed relationship to casual sex.

☐ It's unfeminine to initiate or take the lead during sex.

☐ Women can be and often are as sexually proactive/independent/ dominant as men.

☐ The notion of women as passive sexual creatures is an out-dated stereotype.

☐ Women should have total freedom to express themselves sexually.

☐ All women are different and it's difficult to make generalizations.

☐ Men and women are the same – any differences are culturally conditioned.

To read about pushing back the boundaries during sex go to pages 106–107.
To read about exploding sexual myths go to pages 108–109.

BODY IMAGE

Which of these statements best sum up your attitude to your body?

- [ ] I'm happy with my body.
- [ ] There are things I'd like to change but, generally, I accept my body the way it is.
- [ ] There is a/are specific part/s of my body that I feel self-conscious about.
- [ ] I don't like my partner seeing me naked.
- [ ] I avoid certain sexual positions/acts because I'm inhibited about my body.
- [ ] I dislike my body so much that it stops me enjoying sex.
- [ ] I don't have sex because I feel too unattractive.

To read about ways to improve your body image go to pages 24–5.
To read about relaxing during sex go to pages 66–7.
To read about how sex therapy can help you to overcome inhibitions go to pages 128–31.

ORGASM

Which of these statements describe your orgasms?

- [ ] I climax easily.
- [ ] I find it difficult to climax.
- [ ] I can climax during masturbation but not during intercourse.
- [ ] I have never had an orgasm.
- [ ] Orgasms are an integral part of sex. I feel cheated if I don't have one.
- [ ] Orgasms are optional for me during sex. Sometimes I want one, sometimes I don't.
- [ ] The only/easiest way I can have an orgasm during sex is by touching myself.
- [ ] I need to make love in a certain position to have an orgasm.
- [ ] My partner doesn't touch me in the way that I need during sex.
- [ ] I sometimes/always fake orgasm.

To read about orgasm in detail go to pages 70–73.
To read about sexual positions that enhance female orgasm go to pages 140–43.

SEXUAL CONFIDENCE

Which of these statements describe your level of confidence in bed?

- [ ] If I don't get what I need in bed I generally know how to ask for it.
- [ ] I prefer to guide my partner physically rather than give him verbal instructions.
- [ ] I sometimes put up with things that I'm not happy with in bed.
- [ ] I'm happy to take a dominant role during sex.
- [ ] I'm happy to take a passive role during sex.
- [ ] I usually feel too embarrassed to take the lead in bed.
- [ ] I'm happy to seduce my partner.
- [ ] I feel shy about initiating sex.

To read about asking for what you want during sex go to pages 98–9.
To read about adopting a more exploratory attitude to sex go to Chapter 6.

EXPLORE YOUR BODY

I once knew a woman who refused to let her partner see her naked. She changed into a nightdress in the bathroom and insisted on making love in the dark. She believed that if her partner saw her naked he would find her so repugnant that he would withdraw his love entirely. Eventually he did withdraw, but for a different reason – because he couldn't stand the lack of trust and intimacy between them.

The challenge for all of us is to accept our bodies the way they are now – not when we have lost some weight or worked out at the gym, but now – today! I believe that if we are all hung up on some mythical ideal body this will have a direct impact on our sex lives. After all, you can't immerse yourself in sensual and erotic bliss if you're worried about the flab on your belly. One of the great secrets of being sexy is having confidence in your own body and being obviously at home in it, whether you are 17 or 70, bald or hairy, skinny or overweight. What is unsexy is constant self-awareness or trying to manoeuvre yourself into a position that will conceal a hated part of your body or

refusing to do something in bed because you feel too fat/ugly/old.

Here's a question for you: last time you had mind-blowing sex did you find yourself making mental notes about the appearance of your partner's body, or did you just go with the moment and let yourself be carried away by fantastic sensations? Exactly! Here are two exercises to help you get comfortable with your body.

THE OIL EXERCISE

Reserve an hour of total solitude in the privacy of your bedroom to massage yourself. Start by lying down and doing some deep-breathing exercises (see pages 66–7). Now rub plenty of massage oil into the palms of your hands and simply stroke your body. You don't need to use formal massage strokes. Your aim is to experience how your body feels to the touch. Note the shape, consistency and texture of every part, including the bits of your body you don't like. Visualize the pleasure a lover would get from running his/her hands over your body.

THE MIRROR EXERCISE

Stand in front of a full-length mirror in daylight and look at your body unjudgmentally. Start with the top of your body and work down, then use a handheld mirror to view the back of your body. The aim of this exercise is to stop reacting to your body in habitually negative ways. Describe each part of your body to yourself (either mentally or out loud). For example, you might say, "My nipples look dark against the white skin of my breasts. My belly sticks out a little bit. I like the way my waist is so curvy."

If pejorative words such as "fat" or "horrible" form in your mind, try to replace them with neutral or positive ones such as "soft" or "voluptuous". Tell yourself that your body is the physical history of your life. Remember all the forces that have shaped its appearance, from the time you fell off your bike at the age of five to the children you have had (for example). You can also do this exercise with a partner. Take it in turns to describe each other's bodies in positive terms – you may feel self-conscious at first but it can be a profoundly liberating experience.

I've often been asked what tricks, techniques or chat-up lines will be guaranteed to seduce someone. Of course the disappointing answer is that there aren't any. Having said this, those people who tend to be successful romantically are those who are open to others, those who make us feel listened to and accepted, and those who are at ease with physical intimacy and generous with their affection.

In this chapter we look at how simple things such as talking and listening, observing someone's body language, making romantic gestures and touching someone mindfully can make you a skilled and sensitive lover and partner.

2 SEDUCTION

THE LANGUAGE OF ATTRACTION

How can we tell whether a prospective partner finds us attractive and how do we let them know that we find them sexy? Here, we explore the non-verbal and verbal aspects of the language of attraction.

NON-VERBAL SIGNALS

The language of attraction is unmistakable and universal. For example, we can all spot a couple flirting with each other at a party – the man leans in close to the woman, she takes a sip from her glass without breaking eye contact with him, he smiles, she smiles back and then he says something that makes them both laugh. They move even closer together and she touches his arm.

If you know the secrets of non-verbal communication it's easy to tell when another person finds you sexy. The signs to look out for are proximity (someone seeks you out and stands close to you), sustained eye contact, smiling and, occasionally, an exaggerated interest in what you say. You should also look out for what psychologists call "mirroring" – the

unconscious copying of your postures and movements – and ''preening'', which includes actions such as hair stroking, smoothing clothes down or loosening a tie.

The early cues that people give to you about attractiveness are vitally important, and you need to reciprocate them quickly if you want the flirtation to move on or ignore them if you're not interested.

THE ART OF CONVERSATION

Also important is the conversation that you have with your prospective partner – it doesn't matter so much what you say, but how and when you say it. A good conversation is a subtle interplay of speaking and listening so that you both have a chance to express yourselves and learn something of value about the other person. This means being an attentive and thoughtful listener, using non-verbal signals such as nods and smiles to demonstrate interest, judging the right time to take over the conversation and how long to speak for. It also means speaking at the right speed in a pleasant tone.

KEY CONVERSATION RULES

Next time you feel attracted to someone you are talking to and you want to show it, try the following:

- Concentrate on what the other person is saying and ask questions that show that you're thinking about what they have said.
- Be empathetic. Offer experiences and insights from your own life that demonstrate that you know what they're talking about.
- If you find something funny, let it show.
- Gauge the level of intimacy the other person is striving for and try to match it when it's your turn to speak.
- Strike a balance between friendliness and being awe-struck: don't agree with everything someone says or laugh hysterically at the smallest joke.
- Never try to compete in a conversation.
- If you need to leave the conversation, however briefly, say something like, "Please don't go away, I'll be straight back."
- Pay simple but honest compliments, such as "I've really enjoyed talking to you."

ROMANTIC RITUALS

The process of falling in love must be one of the most heady and intoxicating experiences that life has to offer. Couples in the first throes of love are swamped in romance – an important ingredient in good sex. It's later on in relationships – when you start to notice that your partner has faults just like everyone else – that working at romance becomes a necessity.

Contrary to popular belief, you can't stay in love forever. Most people manage to sustain that special "love-high" for six months to a year. When it eventually wears off, the mistake many people make is to panic, tell themselves that they have fallen out of love and break up. The truth is that, although the next stage of a relationship may be less breath-taking, it offers a great deal in terms of contentment, emotional stability and day-to-day happiness. As long as you remember romance ...

WHAT ROMANCE MEANS

To many people romance means red roses, chocolates and candlelit dinners. If these things work for you, that's great. But another way of approaching romance is to tailor your gestures to your partner's needs and tastes. This could mean giving your partner a book by his favourite writer or making her sandwiches to take to work when you know she's too busy to take a lunch break. If you don't like the word "romance", use "thoughtfulness" instead. A romantic gesture is anything that says "I love and care for you".

Here are two tips. Firstly, gestures that are difficult to accomplish or that involve tastes opposite to your own often feel the most special. For example, if you loathe ironing, offering to press your partner's outfit before she goes out effectively says "I love you enough to make the effort". Secondly, romantic gestures that are continually varied show that you're really thinking about your partner's needs rather than doing things reflexively.

Having said this, don't forget that all the romantic gestures in the world are no substitute for physical affection. When we are touched, held and kissed on a daily basis, this makes us feel loved and sexually alive.

DATING YOUR PARTNER

Go on a date with your partner – go anywhere you like as long as it's just the two of you, you have an uninterrupted day or evening together and you spend at least some of the time talking. Being in a neutral environment away from home allows you to escape from your daily routine and avoid distractions. Make a point of dressing up and looking nice. Charm each other – do anything that will make you feel that this time is special and important.

New lovers ask each other endless questions in an attempt to learn everything they can. In established relationships this kind of talking gets neglected because we make the mistake of thinking we know everything about our partner. On your date, make the effort to connect with your partner by asking questions about what he/she has been thinking about recently. Resist getting bogged down in the minutiae of day-to-day life and try to focus on broader issues: your feelings about the future, your disappointments, your ambitions – the kinds of things that you don't normally talk about.

(This page) Making love on a chair is a wonderful blend of the spontaneous and the erotic, and offers an exciting alternative to making love on a bed. Facing the man, the woman straddles him and guides his penis into her vagina. Her feet are firmly on the ground enabling her to lift herself on and off his penis at whatever pace she likes. He can use his hands to caress her breasts or guide her pace by gripping her waist. Deep kissing in this position adds an extra frisson to the sex. (Opposite) This variation on a woman-on-top position enables the woman to lean back against the man's legs. He lies on his back with knees bent and his feet planted firmly on a wall. The woman straddles the man and lets him take her body weight on his thighs. She can touch her clitoris while he touches her breasts, or vice versa. This is a good position for female orgasm when the man has already ejaculated.

FOODS OF LOVE

Food can add a delicious sensuality to sexual encounters. The very act of eating is often reminiscent of oral sex – think about breaking open a plump, ripe fig and sucking out the contents, or nibbling the top of an asparagus tip that is dripping with butter. Some foods are seductive just by virtue of their appearance and smell – take oysters, for example. Even feeding your partner food from a spoon promotes intimacy by taking you back to the safe, nurturing world of childhood when all your needs were met by a loving parent.

Sharing a meal is a time-honoured way to make us feel romantic and intimate prior to lovemaking, especially if one partner has gone to the effort of preparing something special. Some couples consider eating an essential part of foreplay. You can make a meal extra-sexy by eating with your fingers, letting the juices run over your fingers and chin, and gazing into your partner's eyes suggestively. The message that you're sending is "I want to eat you too!" If this doesn't appeal to you, try popping bite-sized morsels into each other's mouths. You can also move a piece of food such as a cherry back and forth using your lips and tongues.

MIDNIGHT FEAST

This is a special kind of picnic for you and your partner to share in bed. Forget about being sensible and pick foods that you can have fun with: preferably those that are juicy, saucy, fragrant, phallic, or red and succulent, such as cherries, raspberries or strawberries. Also essential is a pot of cream. If you're sweet-toothed, go for chocolate and ice cream. If you're hungry, go for cream cheese and bagels. Lay it all out on your bed and take turns to practise seductive eating (show him how you'd give a blow job on a banana; show her your best tongue techniques on a split-open plum). Later, when you're really aroused, try incorporating food into foreplay by, for example, drizzling cream over her breasts and then licking it off, nibbling a bagel from around his penis or pouring cold champagne over her pubic mound so that it trickles over her clitoris. Be imaginative and, above all, don't worry about the mess!

SLOWING IT DOWN

When we imagine hot, passionate sex we tend to think of ripping each other's clothes off and making love in a mad frenzy of desire. I'd like to challenge the notion that good sex has to be done at a fast pace – I think that some of the most intense sexual experiences come from slowing things right down.

A slow approach works best when you really concentrate on physical sensation. Imagine that you have just received a wonderful massage and you are lying on a bed in a warm room with your eyes closed. Your whole body is alive and tingling with anticipation as you wait to find out what your lover is going to do next. Then you feel his index finger gently touch the top of your neck, just below your hairline. Slowly and softly he traces a line down the entire length of your spine until his finger comes to rest just above the cleft of your buttocks. Even though he hasn't touched you anywhere near your genitals you have just felt the most thrilling sensations imaginable, not just on your back but radiating throughout the core of your body.

The reasons this feels so great are, first, you've got the time to really savour physical touch and, second, you feel relaxed enough to lie back, let go of all worldly distractions and float away on waves of physical pleasure.

Everyone should make time for this kind of build-up to sex. You may not be able to do it every night, or even every week, but you can definitely reserve a one- or two-hour slot once a month to have sex that is slow, languorous and sensual and that allows you literally to get back in touch with your partner.

HOW TO RELAX

To get into a relaxed mood, take turns to perform this simple massage on each other. If you are the person doing the massaging, ask your partner to undress and then kneel down on the floor and rest her chest and upper body on a big stack of cushions or a beanbag. You kneel behind her and rest your hands on either side of the lower part of her spine where her sacrum is (we all harbour a lot of tension here). Start by applying gentle pressure to her sacrum and then move your palms in big, firm, slow circles on her lower back. Ask her to concentrate on breathing deeply. Make the circles bigger and then smaller again. Vary the pressure. Finally, using your fingertips, apply static pressure on either side of her lower spine and tell her to consciously relax this area.

SLOW-SEX TECHNIQUES

When you are both feeling relaxed you can start building up to sex. Slow-sex techniques consist of the simplest types of touch imaginable. Try any or all of the following: hold his penis or her clitoris in your mouth without moving; hold his penis firmly in your hand or press your fingers firmly against the front wall of her vagina for seconds at a time; blow on her breasts or belly, or on his testicles; walk your middle and index fingers up and down the back of her neck and scalp; use a feather-light fingertip touch to stroke his eyelids, earlobes and lips. When – or if – you get round to intercourse, keep your movements deliberately slow and try to feel every tactile nuance of every stroke.

The place in which you regularly make love can play an important role in your sex life. When seeking to create an atmosphere conducive to good sex, take into account all the factors that impact on your senses: smells, sounds, textures, lights – even the visual aesthetics of your decor.

SPACE

I've always thought that the ideal room for sex is one that contains nothing but four walls and a bed. Anything else, such as alarm clocks, chests of drawers, wardrobes, laundry baskets and, worst of all, computers and telephones, drag our attention back to daily life, domesticity and all the jobs that we should be doing.

If you can't have a dedicated sex room, work with what you've got. Rooms that inspire us to have carefree sex are clean and clutter-free, with plenty of room to roll/jump/lie/writhe around in. Even if you start off in the bed it's nice to have the option of moving onto the floor and rolling around on a soft carpet (or vice versa). So try to rationalize your clutter, or, if your bedroom is simply too small to give you a feeling of space, spread some cushions, blankets and duvets on the living room floor and make love there instead.

THE EMOTIONAL IMPACT OF SMELL

Creating a beautiful fragrance is a great subliminal way to shift your mood from downbeat to upbeat or from neutral to sensual. The subtle smells of plant essential oils can wake you up (lemon or rosemary), relax you (lavender or rose) or put you in a sexy/sensual mood (jasmine or ylang ylang). Vaporize oils in a burner or sprinkle a few drops on a light bulb or radiator. Essential oils or – even better – incense, can lend an exotic ambiance to a room (useful if you're going for a *Kama Sutra* atmosphere).

LIGHT AND SOUND

Don't underestimate the impact of light on your mood. Whenever possible make love in natural or candle light or use soft lamps beside the bed. And don't forget that, occasionally, making love in the anonymity of complete darkness can be a powerful turn-on.

INDULGING THE SENSES

Sounds are important too – you can't lose yourself in sex if telephone, traffic or television sounds are impinging on your senses. If you can't eliminate noise, then cover it up with a non-intrusive piece of music, ideally something with personal or romantic resonance. Some people say they find the gentle tinkling of wind chimes conducive to lovemaking.

TEXTURES AND AESTHETICS

Try to create a sensual environment that matches the season: cool, crisp sheets in summer and layers of shawls, blankets and throws to inspire cosy sex in winter.

It's also worth spending time considering the energy of your bedroom. How do you feel when you walk in: happy, sad, relaxed or stressed? Does the room have positive or negative associations for you? Even something as simple as the presence of a mirror can enhance or detract from your lovemaking, depending on how much of an exhibitionist you are.

Colour is also important. Bold, visceral colours, such as deep reds, purples and pinks, are notorious for inspiring passion. Colour therapists say that red in particular increases our blood pressure and heart rate and makes us feel excited – it is the colour of drama and passion. The link between sex and the colour red is even embedded in our language in the form of expressions such as "scarlet woman" and "red-blooded male". Try using a red light bulb – if you don't own one, you can achieve the same effect by filtering light through red fabric.

Rich and warm colours, such as gold and orange, are very sensual. Cold colours, such as white and blue, create a much more sterile ambiance. But, before you decide to paint your bedroom walls crimson, consider the fact that this is also the place in which you have to fall asleep and wake up. One way to create a room that can function both as an exotic boudoir and as a restful haven is to use extravagant accessories – try placing red, velvet cushions, pink roses, purple throws and gold-painted candles around the room – while keeping the basis of the decoration neutral. When you want to relax you can simply strip out the accessories.

If I had to name one indispensable skill when it comes to sex it would be the art of sensual touch. By this I mean the ability – and the imagination – to induce delicious feelings not just in your partner's genitals but all over his or her body from the ear lobes to the big toes. An equally valuable skill is to be able to receive erotic sensations in a mindful way without other feelings and thoughts competing for your attention.

These are skills that can be learned. In this chapter I set out a series of ideas and exercises from massage to meditation to breathing that will help you to hone your sensual awareness. Hopefully, you will set out on a tactile voyage of discovery. You don't need to be thin or beautiful; you don't need expensive lingerie or exotic sex toys; you just need a spirit of openness and the confidence to explore and experiment.

3 SENSATION

THE EROGENOUS SURVEY

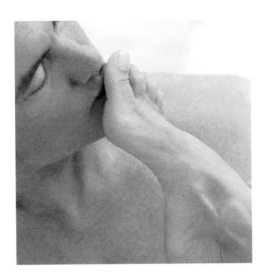

I often hear people complain that there is something missing when sex focuses exclusively on the genitals. One of my female clients said that for a long time her boyfriend didn't know where her clitoris was; then, when she finally plucked up courage to show him, he gave up on the rest of her body. He mistakenly thought that the clitoris was a magic button that would invariably provide a fast-track route to sexual ecstasy. Unfortunately, my client is someone who wants sex to be a whole-body experience and her partner's new "clitocentric" approach left her cold.

Everyone has a part of their body that shivers with pleasure when it is touched in a certain way. Maybe you like having your ear lobes nuzzled, your neck nibbled, your buttocks scratched or your toes sucked. Sex, at its most sublime, is an experience that arouses all sorts of sensations in all sorts of disparate body parts. Even the simplest caress can cause the release of chemicals such as endorphins and oxytocin, which in turn create a delicious physical high. Add orgasm to this equation and

lovemaking can become truly transcendent! But first you need to discover – or rediscover – you and your partner's erogenous zones.

CONDUCTING THE SURVEY

Lie down naked in a warm room with your partner and take it in turns to touch each other all over for around 15 to 30 minutes each. Don't feel you have to use formal massage techniques, and aim to keep your touching sensual rather than sexual by avoiding the genitals. The aim is not to have sex, but to awaken your body to the subtleties of sensual touch.

Experiment with different types of touch on different parts of the body. For example, you could start by kissing or licking the eyelids, running your index finger over your partner's lips, gently pulling the hair or brushing your fingernails against the skin on the back of the neck. As you work your way down the body you could try licking and blowing the skin on the chest (not the breasts), moving your hands in soft, slow circles on the belly and tracing a single line along the inner arm across

the surface of the palm and all the way along the middle finger. Pay lots of attention to parts of the body that you wouldn't normally touch: for example, the armpits, the backs of the knees, the ankles and the spaces in between the toes. Explore different tempos and pressures of touch and use your body as a massage tool in its own right. Exploit not just your hands and tongue, but also your lips, teeth, hair, feet, fingernails, knuckles – you can even use your elbows and eyelashes!

The partner who is being touched should give plenty of verbal feedback – including appreciative noises and moans of pleasure – as well as guidance, such as "faster", "slower", "harder" or "softer".

By the way, if you believe in the myth that good lovemaking should consist only of self-assured techniques that produce instant results you may find this exercise difficult. The erogenous survey is by nature tentative and speculative – it depends on your willingness to go back to basics, to experiment and to learn from your partner.

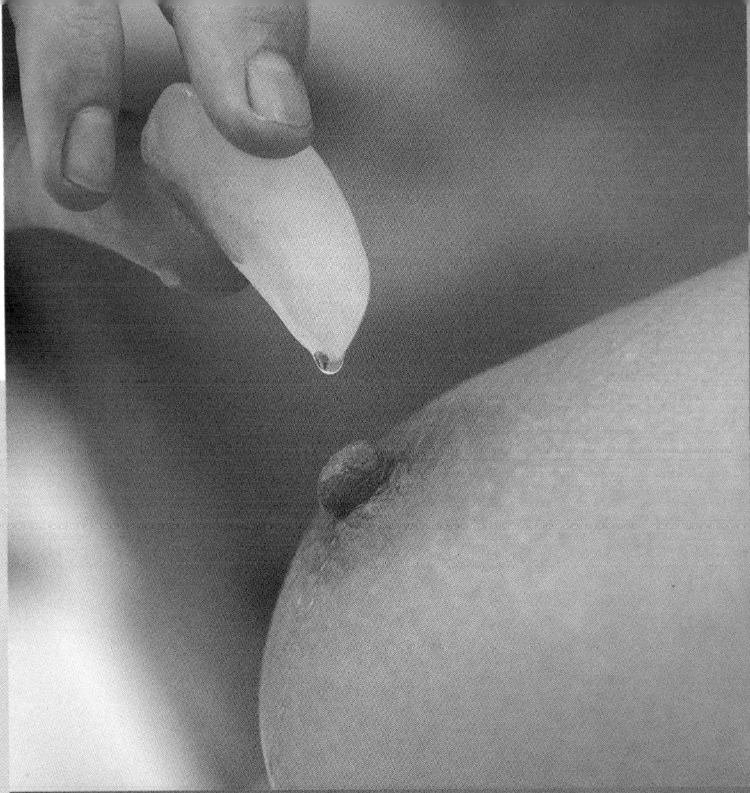

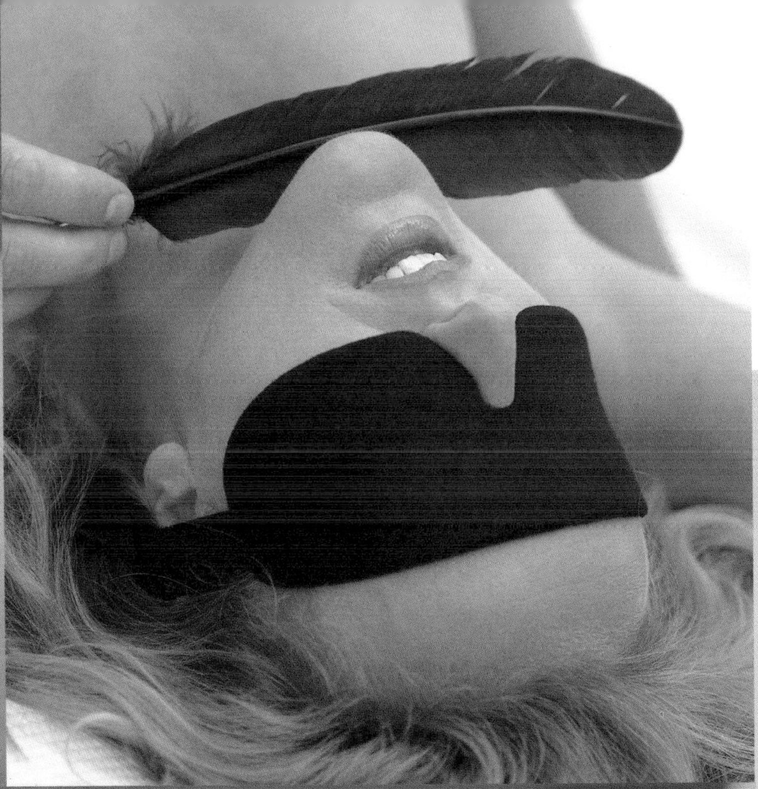

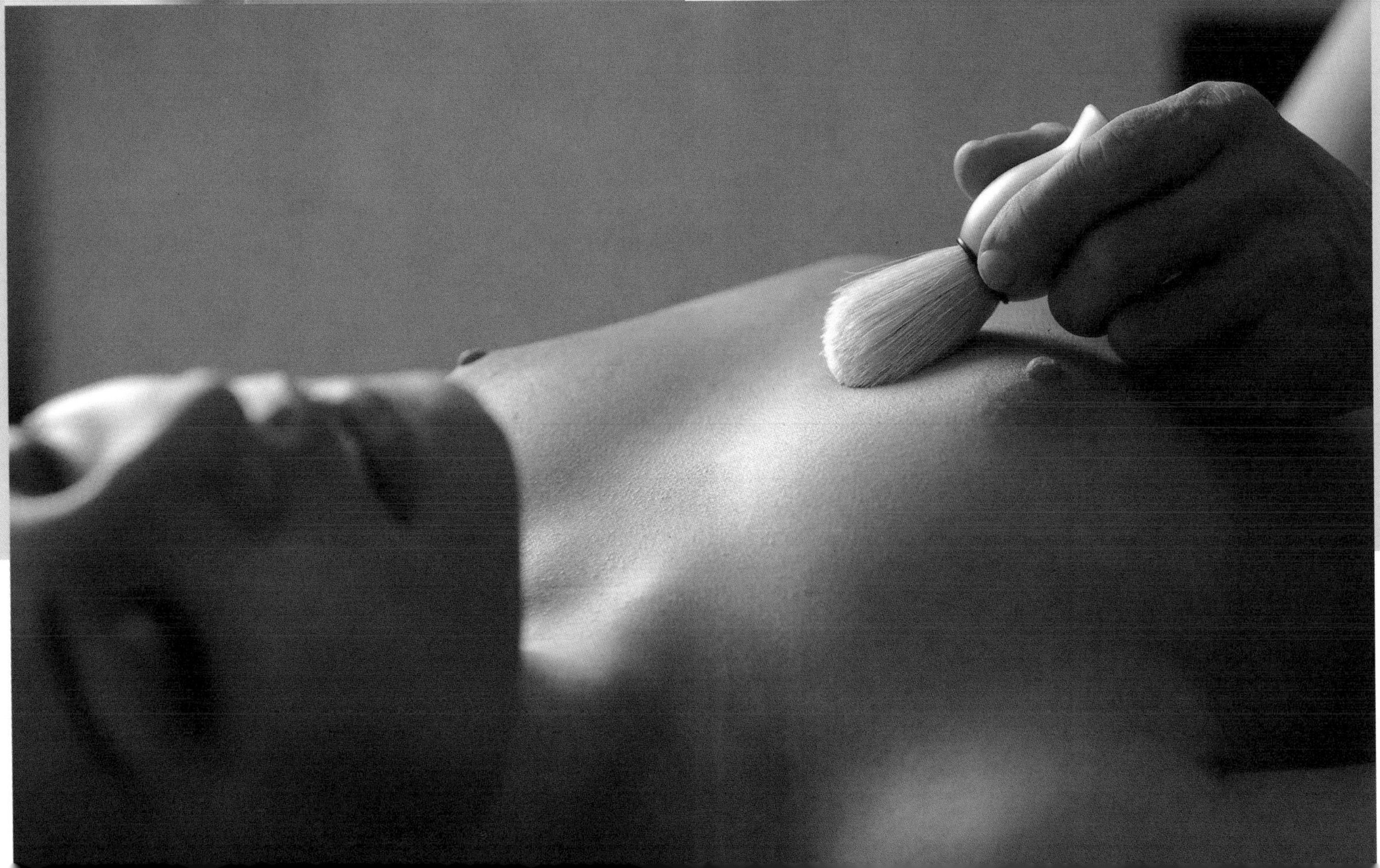

THE SENSUAL TOY-BOX

I believe that we can rediscover our sensuality by indulging in play. One idea is to make a sensual toy-box. This involves seeing the things around you as sensual objects. For example, a string of beads could be used to massage your neck, a tennis ball could stimulate the arches of your feet, a furry paint roller could deliver a unique back massage. Collect a diverse array of objects, get together with your partner and spend some time playing with your new toys. Sexual pleasure isn't crucial. Finding interesting ways of touching each other is!

FROM SILK TO RUBBER

Fabrics can be an integral part of your toy-box. How does a piece of fur/velvet/silk/satin/leather feel on your skin? What about other textures, such as rubber? Which parts of your body are best at detecting different fabrics and textures? Your lips and fingertips have a dense concentration of nerve endings, but can you train other parts of your body – your feet, for example – to be good touch detectives? Blindfold your partner and have fun trying.

THE BEAUTY OF BRUSHES

Brushing the skin can be exquisite or energizing depending on the type of brush you use. Experiment with tiny make-up brushes and the biggest, bristliest paint brushes. Use the small brushes to tease sensitive areas of the body, such as the insides of the thighs or the genitals. Use the big, stiff brushes to stimulate large, muscly areas such as the buttocks. Keep the other person guessing – if you're using a hairbrush on your partner you can flip it round and use it to deliver a gentle, playful spank!

WATER PLAY

Water is a bizarre thing to include in a toy-box, but I'm mentioning it because it has so many different sensual properties: warm water relaxes us; cold water invigorates us; and ice can make us gasp with a mixture of pain and pleasure. Try giving your partner a water massage by using a forceful shower spray to draw circles on his back and buttocks; wash each other in a warm, fragrant and soapy bath; or kiss your partner's body with an ice-cube in your mouth.

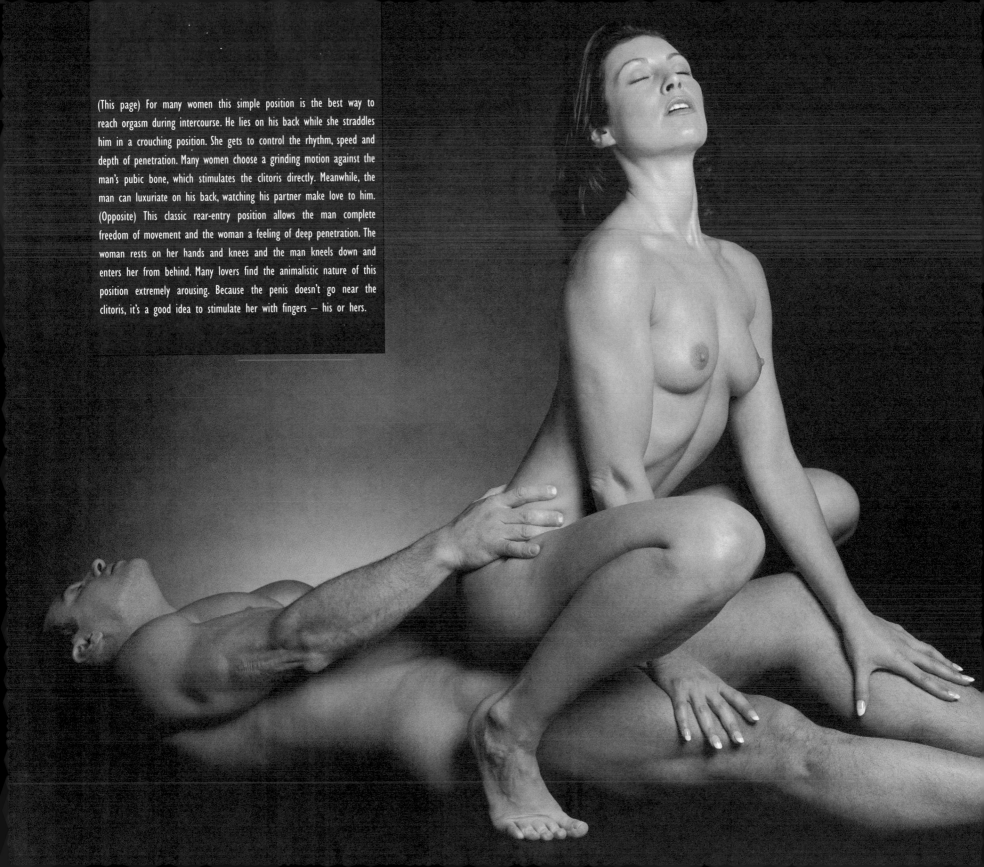

(This page) For many women this simple position is the best way to reach orgasm during intercourse. He lies on his back while she straddles him in a crouching position. She gets to control the rhythm, speed and depth of penetration. Many women choose a grinding motion against the man's pubic bone, which stimulates the clitoris directly. Meanwhile, the man can luxuriate on his back, watching his partner make love to him. (Opposite) This classic rear-entry position allows the man complete freedom of movement and the woman a feeling of deep penetration. The woman rests on her hands and knees and the man kneels down and enters her from behind. Many lovers find the animalistic nature of this position extremely arousing. Because the penis doesn't go near the clitoris, it's a good idea to stimulate her with fingers — his or hers.

THE SEX DETOX

You can dramatically enhance sexual sensation by going on a short sex detox. In the same way that a dietary detox involves reducing your diet to a few simple foods, my detox plan involves going right back to the basics of physical contact by abstaining from intercourse for a while and concentrating on sensual touch. This frees you from any of the performance pressure associated with erections, orgasms and penetration. Instead, your only responsibility is to rediscover your partner in a playful and tactile way. Then, gradually, you reintroduce elements of your sex life one by one, leaving penetrative sex and orgasm until last.

The sex detox will allow you to let go of all your habitual ways of making love so that you can learn new and exciting ways of relating to one another. Here are the exercises – when practising the first three, take it in turns to touch each other.

THE EROGENOUS SURVEY

I have described in detail how to do this first stage on pages 44–5. The important thing to remember during this phase of the detox is that you must not touch each other's genitals (and men must not touch their partner's breasts), because you are not aiming to produce an erotic response. Focus your attention on the sensual feelings produced by giving and receiving touch. Do the erogenous survey on three separate occasions. Don't use massage oil (you'll see why later on).

SEXY TOUCHING

During the second stage of the detox you continue to practise the erogenous survey, but now you are allowed to include your partner's genitals (and breasts) in your sensual explorations. Treat the genitals as just another part of the body to touch and explore (see pages 54–7), and don't try to give your partner an orgasm – it helps if you intersperse genital touching with touching the rest of the body. Aim to find out what feels good and what doesn't, and to experiment with new ways of touching each other. It's not a disaster if you do have an orgasm, but at this early stage in the

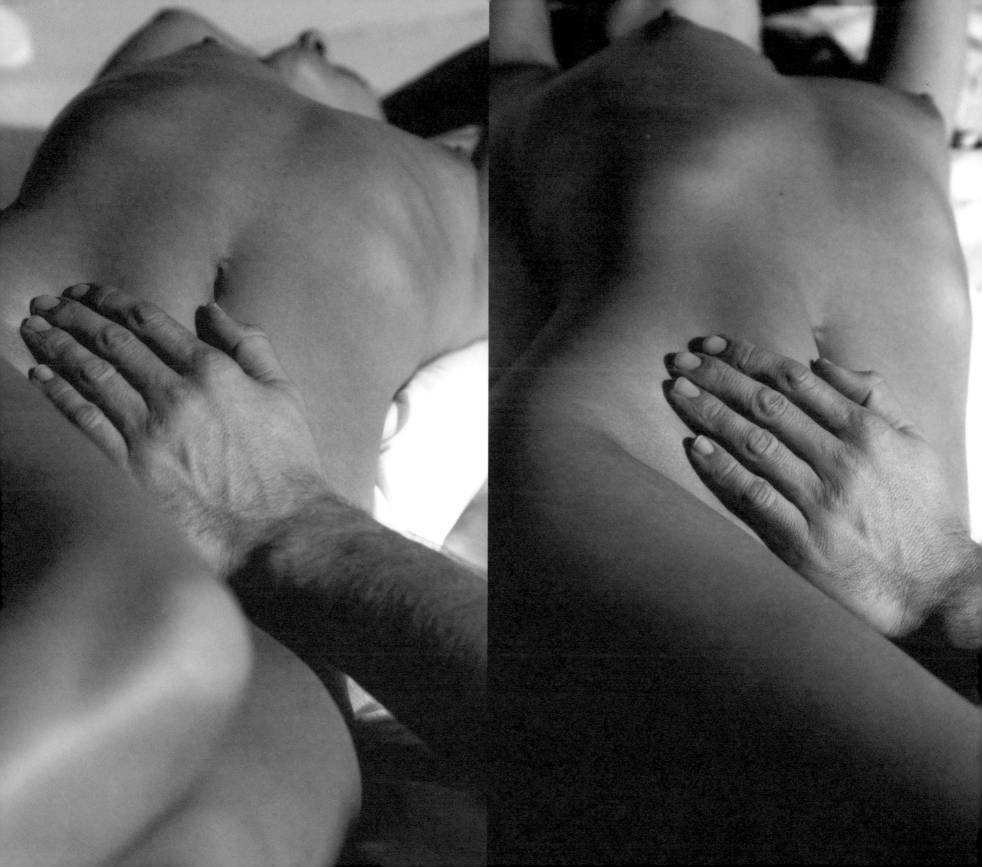

detox it's easy to revert to old sexual habits and this can prevent you from learning new things. Take turns to be the giver and receiver of touch and always offer each other plenty of constructive feedback. Practise sexy touching on three separate occasions.

SLIPPERY TOUCHING

This step is simply an extension of the previous stage, but with the addition of massage oils and genital lubricants. These will help you to enhance and build upon the techniques and sensations you have discovered so far. Practise slippery touching on two separate occasions. You should both continue to try to avoid orgasm.

MUTUAL TOUCHING

Instead of taking it in turns to touch each other, both of you can now apply all the sensual lessons you've learned to mutual touching. Focus on the sensation of simultaneously touching and being touched. Tell each other what you find particularly enjoyable and remember to take everything slowly. Include each other's genitals in your explorations but don't concentrate on them; and be careful not to get so carried away that you have an orgasm or intercourse. Practise mutual touching on three separate occasions.

AND FINALLY ... INTERCOURSE AND ORGASM

Now it's time for penetrative sex and orgasm. Rather than thinking of it as sexual intercourse, instead consider the experience as sensual intercourse, in which you put into practice all the things you have learned from your explorations of each other's body in the previous steps of the sex detox.

Make sure you keep things slow and tactile during this stage. Bring each other to orgasm in any way that you like. He can give her an orgasm with his mouth, lips and tongue before he penetrates her. She can stimulate her clitoris with her hand at the same time as he slowly makes love to her. Or he can make her climax after intercourse – by the time she has had an orgasm he may even start to feel the first stirrings of arousal again.

Couples who follow the sex detox through to this final stage often find that they have a new, unhurried approach to sex: they think nothing of spending as long as an hour on foreplay. Some report that they have more intense orgasms than before because they are able to really give themselves up to sexual pleasure. Others say that sex becomes more of a whole-body experience, or that the emotional aspect of their relationship improves as a result of their heightened sensuality.

Sometimes it can be a wonderful indulgence to receive a sexual massage without any need to reciprocate. It also feels like a fantastic gift from your partner. The massage I've described below incorporates several different types of genital touching and lasts about half an hour – longer if you get carried away.

Start by making sure that the room is warm and comfortable and that you have guaranteed privacy. Both of you should be naked. The person giving the massage should coat his or her hands in plenty of warm massage oil, such as almond oil (please note, if you end up having sex, that oil can damage condoms).

MASSAGE FOR HER

Ask your partner to lie down on her back with her legs apart. Kneel or sit cross-legged between her legs and place one palm on her vulva and one palm between her breasts. Apply fairly firm pressure and leave your hands there for two to three minutes. This is a centring process that allows you to relax and connect with your partner. Breathe deeply into your belly (see pages 66–7) and try to synchronize your breathing with your partner's.

Use these minutes to forget about all the day-to-day worries and preoccupations in your life. Instead, focus on all the loving feelings that you have for your partner. If your thoughts drift in a negative direction and you start to remember unresolved gripes and arguments, make a deliberate effort to think positively. Tell yourself that any differences or disagreements can be set aside for a short period of time. If you find this difficult, remember a time when you and your partner felt intimate and loving and meditate upon this. When you feel ready you can begin your massage.

Using plenty of oil, start to gently pull and squeeze first the outer lips and then the inner lips of your partner's vulva between your thumb and fingers. Now move up to the pubic mound and gently pull and squeeze the fleshy area there. Next, massage your partner's clitoris with your first three fingers, using circular movements. Keep alternating the pressure between feather-light and firm and observe

INTIMATE MASSAGE

your partner's breathing and facial expressions as you do so – these are the best clues to her enjoyment. Now lay your index and middle finger on either side of her clitoris and squeeze them gently together. Keep your clitoral massage slow and paced rather than fast and rhythmic – orgasm isn't your main aim.

Now very gently insert the middle finger of your other hand into your partner's vagina and use it to massage and caress the vaginal walls. Experiment with different depths, speeds and pressures and then try inserting a second or even a third finger into the vagina (as long as your partner finds this comfortable). Pay particular attention to the front wall of the vagina where the G-spot lies (see pages 76–9). If you can, keep doing the clitoral massage with one hand and the vaginal massage with the other. If you find this difficult, instead use the middle finger of your right hand to caress her vagina and your right thumb to caress her clitoris. If you are particularly dextrous you can also use the little finger of your right hand to caress her anus.

Keep massaging your partner for as long as she wants you to. If she has an orgasm, that's fine, but it's not essential. When the massage is over, spend some quiet time lying in each other's arms.

MASSAGE FOR HIM

Ask your partner to lie down on his back. Kneel or sit cross-legged between his legs. Hold his testicles gently in one hand and lay the palm of your other hand on his chest. Breathe deeply together for a few minutes – this will allow you to unwind and connect with each other. Do the loving meditation that I describe at the beginning of Massage for Her.

Now massage your partner's testicles by gently pulling your oiled hands over them repeatedly. This should encourage the whole scrotal area to relax. Next massage his perineum (the area behind his scrotum) by making soft pressing, stroking and circling movements with your fingers.

Hold the base of your partner's penis using your thumb and index finger in a ring shape. Pull this "ring" up the shaft and over the head of his penis. Make the same movement with your other hand. Keep repeating this so that as soon as one hand reaches the top of the penis the other hand encircles the base. As his penis becomes erect you can do this movement with your whole fist instead of just your thumb and index finger. Now use the pad of your thumb to make tiny, gentle circles on the head of his penis. Pay particular attention to his frenulum – the ridge of sensitive skin that joins the glans to the shaft. If you think your partner is going to ejaculate, slow down your massage or turn your attention to another part of his body, such as his chest or thighs. It's OK if he does ejaculate, but it's not the main point of the massage. And don't worry if your partner has an erection and then loses it during the course of the massage. This waxing and waning of the penis is natural and isn't a sign of boredom.

Now return to the perineum. Press gently about halfway between your partner's testicles and anus and ask him if he feels an area of particular sensitivity. This is the prostate gland, which is also known as the male G-spot. Try massaging this area using gentle and then increasingly firm fingertip pressure. In Tantric sex this area is called the "sacred spot" and it can be used for spiritual healing. Your partner may not be used to being touched in this area and some men may feel unexpectedly vulnerable. If this is the case, talk quietly to your partner and ask him what sort of touch is appropriate.

After a minute or two of massaging the perineum, use your other hand to rub your partner's penis up and down again. If you keep doing this, it's highly likely that your partner will ejaculate. If you want him to delay ejaculating as long as possible, use the techniques described on pages 138–9. Alternatively, if you both want to make love at this point, you can. Choose a position that will prolong the mood of intimacy, such as the spoons position, in which you nestle into the front of your partner's curved body (see pages 112–13).

When your massage is finished lie down with your partner and embrace him. Close your eyes and keep your breathing synchronized.

Lie completely still with him inside you and then flex and relax your pelvic floor mucles.

Lubricate your fingers with oil and trace slow, sensual circles around her anus.

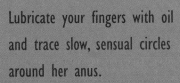

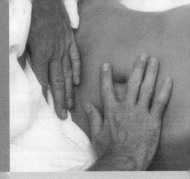

Gently tweak and tug her inner and outer labia, starting at the front and slowly moving back.

Caress her nipples with a feather or a silk scarf.

Try coitus *à la florentine*, in which you draw back his foreskin with your hand and keep it stretched taut for the duration of sex.

Gaze deeply into his eyes while giving him a blow job.

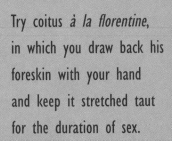

Penetrate her deeply when you are on top by putting a couple of pillows under her buttocks before you begin.

When you are on top of him, reach down and gently fondle his balls.

Use your hand to flick the head of your penis back and forth over her clitoris until she comes.

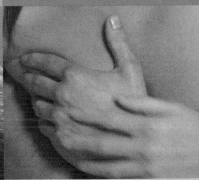

Lick the head of his penis as if it were an ice-cream then stop and gently breathe out as if you were steaming up a mirror.

Lightly graze his buttocks with your fingernails when he's on top of you.

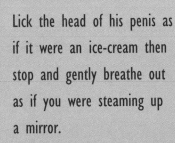

Use a vibrator on his anus just as he's about to come.

Tease him by squatting above him and bobbing up and down on the tip of his penis.

After you've made love tell each other exactly what you enjoyed about it and be as specific as you can.

50 WAYS TO PLEASE YOUR LOVER

Make the shape of the letter X. She sits astride him and then lies back and stretches her legs out. Each partner's head is between the other's feet.

Try the scissors position: lie facing each other on your sides; her leg goes on top, then his leg, then her leg, then his leg.

Lay a full-length mirror on the floor and then make love doggy-style over the top of it.

Try using each other's feet as sex toys. Kiss and lick them and use your toes to bring each other to orgasm.

Let him get really deep inside you by bringing your knees to your chest and resting your ankles on his shoulders.

Stroke her clitoris through fabric such as silk.

Try kinky mutual masturbation — wear gloves. Rubber, leather or lace!

Make her come through hand-riding. You put your hand on her clitoris and she moves it in the rhythm she likes best.

Wait until she gets the first contractions of orgasm and then massage her G-spot with your fingers.

Penetrate her as deeply as you can and then wiggle your hips from side to side.

Kneel back on your heels supporting yourself with your hands and then get her to sit astride you.

Dedicate an evening to doing exactly what your partner asks you to do in bed — with no holds barred.

Try to make love without breaking eye contact.

Let your lover watch you undress and have a shower. Then invite him/her in for sex standing up.

Give each other an erotic surprise: travel on an overnight sleeper train, visit a sauna or book a hotel room for the weekend.

Strip, cover each other in oil and let your bodies slip and slide against each other.

Make your bedroom pitch-black and have fun slowly exploring your lover's body by torchlight.

Write 10 sex positions on strips of paper and put them in a jar. Pull one out each time you make love.

Whisper "I want you now" when you're out together. Then find somewhere discreet to make love.

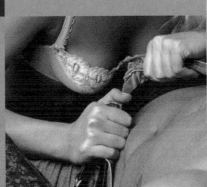

Take turns to masturbate in front of each other.

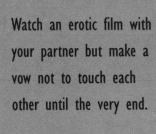

Watch an erotic film with your partner but make a vow not to touch each other until the very end.

Suck his fingers as he makes love to you.

Invent sexy roles for each other, such as lap dancer, dominatrix or slave, and act them out.

Try the wheelbarrow. She supports herself on the floor on her forearms. He kneels on the floor, puts her legs around his waist and penetrates her.

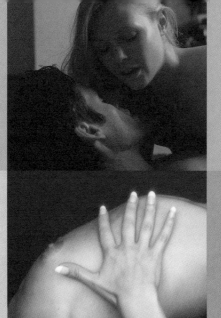

Next time you're apart for the night make a date to have phone sex.

Have a bath in which you take it in turns to soap, wash and dry each other — with particular emphasis on the erogenous zones.

During oral sex lightly graze him with your teeth, suck a menthol sweet or use your hand on the base of the shaft and your tongue on the tip.

Make each other come with all your clothes on.

Bite each other! Start with gentle nibbles on the earlobes, neck or buttocks and then explore further.

Wear nothing but lip gloss to bed and let him spend ages kissing it off.

Don't make love for a week, or longer, and then have a night of sexual indulgence, preferably away from home.

Find somewhere private and make as much noise as you can during sex. Express your feelings through moans, groans, pants, sighs, yells and screams.

Choose your favourite sex scene from a film and then re-enact it.

Give her a powerful orgasm by rubbing her clitoris, G-spot and anus simultaneously.

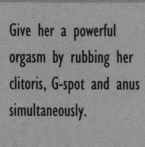

Pick a specific area of the body — not the genitals — and make love to it in all the ways you can think of, using your fingers, lips and tongue.

Give him a hair massage. Straddle him, dip your head forward and use your hair to stroke his chest, belly and penis.

SENSUAL MEDITATION

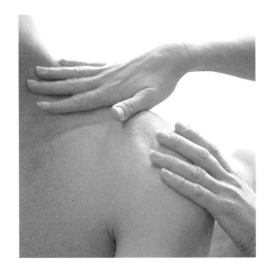

How often do you have mindful sex (see page 70) during which your mind is completely empty of all thoughts and the only thing you're aware of is the erotic sensation you are experiencing? It's an unfortunate fact that many of us usually make love with only half (or less!) of our attention. You can remedy this by practising sensual meditation. Start by sitting naked facing your partner with your eyes closed.

SENSUAL MEDITATION FOR HIM

Place your hands on your partner's shoulders and gently trace their shape with your palms. Bring your hands down onto her chest and feel the way it rises and falls as she breathes in and out. Note whether her breathing is fast and shallow or slow and deep. Now touch her breasts. Rather than turning her on, your aim is to observe the shape and texture of her body; this may sound clinical but it's a superb way of honing your senses. Are her breasts warm or cool, heavy or light, soft or firm? What shape are they? Are her nipples erect? Listen to her breathing – how does it change as you touch

different parts of her breasts in different ways? If you become aroused, ignore it – your sole job at the moment is to observe and explore her body.

Now touch your partner's belly. Note how it moves as she breathes in and out. Gently trace the outline of her navel with your fingertips and enjoy the softness of her skin. Find where her pubic hair starts. Feel its texture – is it fine, silky, coarse or wiry? Touch her genitals with your fingers: explore her clitoris, her inner and outer labia and the opening to her vagina – it's easy to get carried away here, but try to stay with the meditation. You can always make love later on.

SENSUAL MEDITATION FOR HER

Use the palms of your hands to trace the musculature of your partner's upper arms, shoulders and chest. Which areas feel hard and which areas feel softer? How much hair is beneath your fingertips and where does it start and stop? Run your hands over your partner's nipples and note whether they are erect. Now

get your partner to turn around so that you can touch his back. Explore the contours of his muscles. Do his shoulders feel tense or relaxed? Run your hands down his lower back and feel the rising contours of his buttocks. Is this part of his body warm or cool, smooth or hairy, hard or soft?

Return to the front of the body and use your fingers to touch your partner's penis and testicles. Is he erect, flaccid or in-between? Touch him along the length of his penis and feel how his foreskin moves over the shaft. If he is circumcised, gently touch the skin of the glans. Listen to his breathing and note how this changes according to how you are touching him. Now cup his testicles in your hand. Do they feel loose or drawn up tightly to his body? What does the skin feel like to your fingertips? Resist the temptation to get drawn into sex at this point – the idea is that you learn to concentrate on the subtleties of touch. It might help to imagine that you are a blind person trying to memorize all the features of someone else's body with your hands.

(This page) In this pose the combination of proximity and distance is a powerful turn-on. The woman lies on her back and raises her legs at right angles to her body. The man kneels with his legs apart and enters her. This allows for deep penetration and the exquisite sensation of thrusting on the G-spot. (Opposite) The elements of dominance and surrender in this position are compelling. The man picks up the woman and she presses her thighs around his hips and winds her arms around his neck. He then guides his penis into her vagina. He can control the tempo by holding her buttocks and moving her body back and forth.

BELLY BREATHING

If you watch a sex scene in a movie, the lovers will probably gasp, sigh and pant their way to the heights of sexual ecstasy. However, although it's completely natural to breathe fast as you approach orgasm, it's far from essential to puff your way through foreplay. In fact, the slower you breathe during foreplay, the more intense the sexual sensations you are likely to experience.

As yogis have known for centuries, the way that you breathe has a profound effect on your whole state of being. For example, if you take short, shallow, uneven breaths that penetrate only the top part of your lungs, you are likely to feel edgy, anxious and unable to relax. If, on the other hand, you take long, deep, full breaths that go all the way down to your abdomen, you will probably feel at ease and in an open and peaceful state of mind.

THE SENSUAL BREATH

Here are some of the ways that deep, slow, belly breathing can enhance sex:

• We often keep up a mental running commentary during sex. For example: "Mmmm, that feels good ... oh, I'm not so sure about that ... she's not touching me quite right ... oh, no, that's better", and so on. By concentrating on deep breathing you unite your mind and body, bring your awareness back to the present moment and stop behaving like an observer in your own sex life.

• Belly breathing encourages you to feel relaxed. This means that you are more open to sensual sensations and less likely to be suffering from the hang-ups and self-conscious feelings that preoccupy many of us during sex.

• Deep breathing slows down sex, turning it into something long and languorous instead of a goal-orientated rush toward orgasm. This is especially useful for men who get excited very quickly or suffer from premature orgasm, or for women who need a lot of stimulation in order to become aroused.

HOW TO BELLY BREATHE

Place the palms of your hands on your abdomen and inhale deeply through your nose. Draw the breath right down into the centre of your belly so that your abdomen swells and pushes your palms outward. Savour the feeling of the air slowly filling up every part of your lungs. Try to make your inhalation last for a count of 10. Now release your breath slowly, also to a count of 10. Try to keep your inhalations and exhalations deep and flowing. Once you've mastered belly breathing, practise it during sex. Compare the sensations you experience during belly breathing with the way you usually breathe during sex.

WHEN NOT TO BELLY BREATHE

If you are struggling to reach orgasm (more likely if you are a woman), belly breathing can be counterproductive in that it can prevent the build-up of bodily tension that's necessary for you to climax. In the final, orgasmic stages of sex, muscles all over the body tense, your heart rate and blood pressure increase and your breathing accelerates dramatically. So, if you're feeling close to climax, allow yourself to go with the flow. Reserve belly breathing for the delicious, erotic feelings of the early stages of sex.

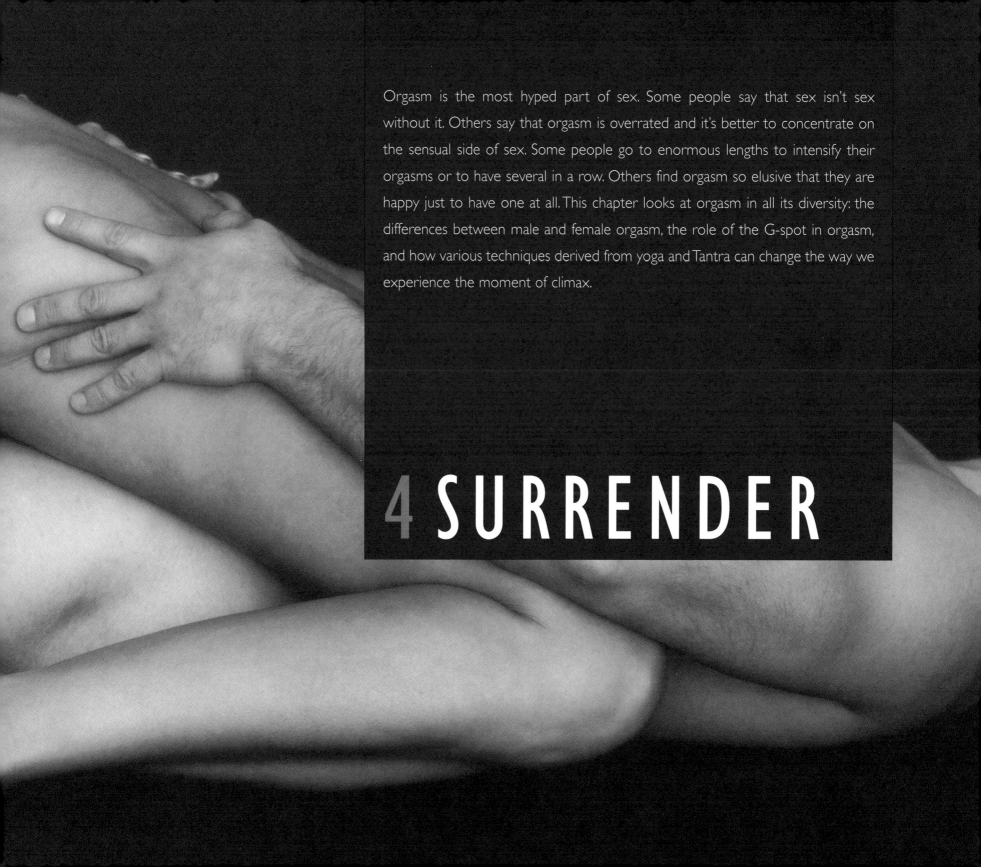

Orgasm is the most hyped part of sex. Some people say that sex isn't sex without it. Others say that orgasm is overrated and it's better to concentrate on the sensual side of sex. Some people go to enormous lengths to intensify their orgasms or to have several in a row. Others find orgasm so elusive that they are happy just to have one at all. This chapter looks at orgasm in all its diversity: the differences between male and female orgasm, the role of the G-spot in orgasm, and how various techniques derived from yoga and Tantra can change the way we experience the moment of climax.

4 SURRENDER

UNDERSTANDING ORGASM

I've read many clinical descriptions of orgasm and there's a wealth of fascinating information available. For example, did you know that the muscles in the vagina and penis both contract rhythmically at intervals of 0.8 seconds during orgasm? Or that men usually experience between three and six consecutive orgasmic contractions, while women can experience up to 12? Were you aware that a woman's uterus rises and the upper part of her vagina expands or "balloons" during orgasm? Or that when a man climaxes the sphincter muscle at the entrance to his bladder closes? Sex researchers have so thoroughly mapped and monitored human sexual responses that, on a physiological level, there is very little that we don't know about orgasm.

But it strikes me that clinical descriptions of orgasm tell only half of the story, and it's not good enough to view orgasm solely as a set of muscular contractions. For many people, it is a profound emotional and even spiritual experience. It can also be a deeply satisfying way of connecting with another person.

THE MIND—BODY CONNECTION

One reason that purely physiological explanations of orgasm are inadequate is that they don't account for the role of the mind during sex. Even if your partner is the most good-looking person in the world or you haven't had sex for a year, your body will still refuse to "let go" if your thoughts are predominately negative. Some of the most common reasons for not being able to perform or climax during sex include anger, anxiety, depression, resentment, guilt and boredom. Even a simple case of nerves can interfere with sex. If you're making love with a new partner, for example, and you're excessively worried about making a good impression, sexual pleasure can easily fly out of the window.

You can help to ensure that you have satisfying sex by acquiring what Buddhists call "mindfulness" — being present in the moment without distraction and being at one with, rather than in opposition to, your body. Anyone who has ever had an orgasm will know what this feeling is like: it's a state of complete

mental and physical immersion when your conscious mind suspends all activity and you enter a state of seeming timelessness. The challenge that all of us face is to learn how to get into this state, not just during the few, fleeting moments of orgasm, but for the entire duration of a sexual encounter – from the first caress to the final embrace. I've written about some of the ways to be mindful during sex in Chapter 3. Belly breathing (see pages 66–7) and meditation (see pages 62–3) are both excellent methods of achieving this state.

MEN VERSUS WOMEN

Although there are many similarities between male and female orgasm there are also some important differences. Most men can reach orgasm with comparative ease. And before they do so they reach a point of "no return" (the clinical name for this is "ejaculatory inevitability"), after which they cannot prevent themselves climaxing. Women, in contrast, tend to be slower to reach orgasm and they don't experience a point of no return, meaning that

they can be distracted from orgasm right up until the last moment.

Another important difference is that the thrusting movement of the penis during intercourse provides the perfect stimulation for men to reach orgasm but doesn't do the same for women because it fails to provide friction on the clitoris. This is why most women need additional clitoral touching to have an orgasm during intercourse.

To truly understand the differences between male and female orgasm you need to talk in depth with your partner about it. This means really getting down to the nitty gritty of what you do together in bed. So, for example, he could ask her whether she likes her clitoris to be touched directly/indirectly approaching and during orgasm – and at what speed and what pressure – and whether she enjoys her breasts and vagina being touched during orgasm. She could ask him how she can make his orgasms as intense as possible. Should she stay still and let him move or does he find it erotic when she does all the work? What kind of touch does he like immediately before, during and after he climaxes? For example, does he enjoy having his nipples or testicles caressed?

VAGINA VERSUS CLITORIS

There is much hype about the different types of female orgasm and whether or not one type is superior to another. This is a debate that started with Sigmund Freud, who postulated that there were two types of female orgasm: the clitoral orgasm – which he claimed is a sign of sexual immaturity – and the vaginal orgasm – which supposedly represents sexual maturity. Today the range of possible orgasms includes not just clitoral and vaginal but also multiple, sequential and simultaneous orgasm, not to mention female ejaculation. My opinion – and one which is shared by the majority of sex therapists – is that all types of orgasm are as valid as each other. What is really important is that you and your partner find the sexual expression that best suits you as individuals. Above all, don't waste time striving to achieve something elusive, such as simultaneous

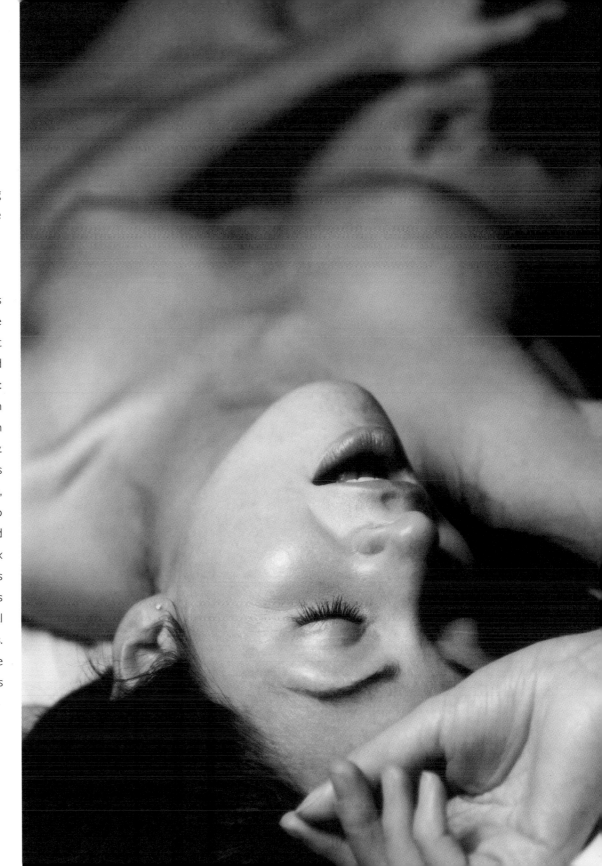

orgasm, just because you think it sounds good. Goal-orientated sex that puts both of you under pressure is always a bad idea.

IS ORGASM ESSENTIAL?

Some people say that sex can be complete without orgasm and I would agree with them – up to a point. The opposing side of the argument is represented by all the women who have experienced extreme frustration in their sex lives because they lack the confidence, the experience or the knowledge to have an orgasm. I've worked with many women who, having learned to become orgasmic through masturbation (and then conveying this knowledge to a partner), have undergone a revolution in their sex lives. So, as with all aspects of sex, you need to find your own sexual style. If you always have orgasmic sex, try changing the focus to something sensually orientated next time you make love. If you never have orgasms and you'd like to, read the section on sexual communication (see pages 98–9) and on intimate genital massage (see pages 54–7).

EXTENDING ORGASM

Although I don't recommend getting too hung up on orgasm, it can be wonderful to prolong those delicious feelings that pervade the genitals and body. It's a well-documented fact that women can have multiple orgasms, but it's less well known that there are techniques that men can use to extend orgasm.

THE MULTI-ORGASMIC WOMAN

The route to female multiple orgasm is simply to continue clitoral touching after you have experienced one orgasm. The clitoris is exquisitely sensitive immediately after climax – some women can "ride it out" so that the sensitive feelings turn into the beginning of the next orgasm; other women find clitoral touching after orgasm verges on being painful and they need to take a break before resuming stimulation. The main thing is to keep touching the clitoris and see what happens! But please be aware that there's a lot of variation in women's experiences of multiple orgasm – some women have a series of gentle, orgasmic waves while others have several steep, sharp climaxes.

Some women are happy with one orgasm, others are happy with 10. As always, it's important to discuss this openly with your partner and experiment together in order to find what's right for you.

THE MULTI-ORGASMIC MAN

Multiple orgasms in men hinge on the ability to experience the muscular contractions of orgasm while holding off from ejaculation. This means that you get to keep your erection and can go on to enjoy repeated orgasms. The US sexologists William Hartman and Marilyn Fithian say that with much practice men can learn how to do this – it all depends on the strength of the pubococcygeal or "PC" muscle and on the man being sensitive to the signs of impending climax.

The first step in the search for multiple orgasms is to strengthen your PC muscle through exercise. You can do this by contracting the area around your anus and perineum (imagine that you are trying to stop yourself urinating). Now relax. Now contract again. The more you do this, the stronger your PC muscle will become. This exercise is very similar to (and interchangeable with) the yogic root-lock exercise I describe on pages 86–7. In fact, all of the male multi-orgasm techniques are borrowed from Tantrism (see pages 82–5). (According to Tantrism, ejaculation leads to a loss of vital energy and should, therefore, be avoided as far as possible.)

The next step is to practise contracting your PC muscle when you feel you are close to orgasm. It's probably easier to do this during solitary masturbation rather than during intercourse at first. Practise deep belly breathing (see pages 66–7) and mindfulness (see pages 62–3) to hone your awareness of your body – increased heart and breathing rates, muscular tension and penile tingling are all signs that climax is near. Now you just need to perfect your timing: let the orgasmic contractions through but then pull up your PC muscle tightly to prevent ejaculation. Hopefully, your erection will still be strong after this and you can repeat the process all over again.

THE G-SPOT

Today we are all accustomed to reading about sex in magazines, newspapers and books. Yet when the G-spot was first "discovered" in the 1940s there was widespread ignorance about sex, and debate among scientists about whether women were even capable of orgasm. So the idea that there was a spot on the front wall of the vagina that could lead to a unique type of sexual pleasure was truly revelatory.

WHAT IS THE G-SPOT?

Ernst Grafenberg was the German obstetrician and gynecologist who noted that there was a specific erogenous zone located on the front wall of the vagina behind the pubic bone and urethra. Stimulating this area could make it swell and produce feelings of sexual pleasure. During the sexual revolution of the 1970s everyone from feminists to gynecologists argued about whether or not the G-spot actually existed. Even now the debate continues, probably fuelled by the fact that some women say they can't find any evidence of a G-spot, while others say that it's an integral part of their sex life.

I think that part of the problem with the G-spot is that women are not encouraged to explore their own genitals. If you were told off for touching yourself as a child, you may be harbouring deep-seated feelings of guilt about self-exploration in adulthood.

Women aren't helped by the position of the G-spot – angling your fingers to reach exactly the right spot can be a tricky business. This problem is compounded by the fact that, if you're not already aroused, the G-spot may not yield any erotic feelings. And some women may naturally lack sensitivity in this area.

MAPPING THE G-SPOT

If you want to have a go at locating your G-spot with your fingers the best idea is to squat down and insert your longest finger into your vagina (this will feel much nicer if you're already aroused). Aim to hit the front vaginal wall about 5 cm (2 inches) up. If you don't feel anything special, don't worry. Just keep applying firm, steady pressure or, if this doesn't work, vibrating pressure. Note that you probably don't need to

reproduce the fast back and forth or circular friction that you would if you were masturbating.

Some women say that the initial sensations of G-spot stimulation resemble the desire to urinate. If you keep applying pressure, however, the feeling becomes more sensual and pleasurable. You may also be able to feel a localized swelling or lump beneath your fingers. Bear in mind that for some women the G-spot exists simply as an awareness that the front wall of the vagina is a bit more sensitive than the back wall.

Instead of using your own fingers to find your G-spot, you may find it easier if your partner uses his, as he has more freedom to manoeuvre. Alternatively there are vibrators (or vibrator attachments) that are specially designed to stimulate the G-spot – they have a curved tip. Another alternative is to explore the G-spot during intercourse – certain sex positions involve the penis thrusting directly against the front wall of the vagina. The best ones are the doggy position, in which the man enters the woman from behind (see pages 48–9), and a

variation of the missionary position in which the woman raises her legs to her chest and puts her feet over the man's shoulders (see pages 64–5). If you try the latter position, experiment with your legs at different angles. See if there is a certain angle at which the thrusting movements of the penis suddenly produce enhanced vaginal sensitivity.

A WORD OF CAUTION

Two myths in circulation are that G-spot stimulation leads to new levels of sexual bliss and that women who have "G-spot orgasms" are sexually superior. I know of at least one woman who became so hung up on the search for her G-spot that she became convinced that she was anatomically abnormal. Both she and her partner were increasingly frustrated and believed that the "normal sex" they were having was inadequate. I think this is an excellent example of the difference between sex that is exploratory and sex that is aspirational. Exploratory sex is done in a spirit of adventure. Aspirational sex aims to be bigger and better

than the sex you are having at the moment and can send you into a frenzy of sexual self-improvement. Don't let your efforts to find your G-spot become stressful. Always follow this simple rule: if it isn't fun, don't do it.

THE MALE G-SPOT

Experts say that if the female G-spot does exist then it's probably analogous to the male prostate gland. The prostate (a gland that encircles the urethra just under the bladder and which produces part of the seminal fluid) is an incredibly sensitive area, the stimulation of which can lead to rapid ejaculation. Men who have anal sex are well acquainted with the prostate, or male G-spot, because the thrusting movements of the penis inside the rectum directly stimulate it. You can also stimulate the prostate gland manually by inserting your lubricated fingers into the rectum and pressing on the front wall. An alternative is to stimulate the prostate gland "remotely" by applying firm pressure to your partner's perineum – the area just behind his testicles and before his anus.

(This page) In this restful position the man lies on his side, thrusting freely, while the woman lies on her back, her legs over his waist so that her body is at right angles to his. Lots of couples find this position useful when the woman doesn't want any weight on top of her — during pregnancy, for example. (Opposite) This is a particularly intimate position in which partners lie facing each other on their sides and the woman clasps or hugs the man with her arms and legs — one leg above his waist and the other underneath. The easiest type of movement is a gentle rocking. To deepen penetration the man can draw his legs up toward his chest.

THE ART OF TANTRA

People tend to get very excited about Tantric sex, probably because of its reputation for secret and exotic methods of inducing sexual bliss. But, like any other spiritual practice, it can't be reduced to a set of tricks or techniques. It takes a long time to learn Tantric sex, and the point of it, rather than having mind-blowing orgasms, is to experience a state of union with your partner and the rest of the universe.

This doesn't mean that we can't adopt some of the principles of Tantric sex without studying it in depth. One of the most interesting divisions between Eastern and Western attitudes to sex is that in the West we tend to think about sex in terms of what we can get out of it. Although the pay-offs are wonderful (physical enjoyment, intimacy with a partner and all the emotional and psychological benefits of feeling loved, needed and desired), Eastern attitudes toward sex are generally far less goal-orientated. Instead, sex is a means of reaching a contemplative and meditative state of mind that elevates you to a state of higher consciousness.

I think it's good for us to know that sex isn't necessarily about being swept away by tidal waves of desire and passion, having throbbing erections that appear on demand and reaching fast, powerful orgasms every time we make love. This is how sex is often depicted in the Western media, and – even if we don't aspire to a higher consciousness – Eastern teachings such as Tantrism can provide us with a refreshing, alternative perspective.

SEXUAL ENERGY

Energy is important in Tantric lovemaking. Not the Western sort of energy that powers us through the day, but the Eastern sort, defined as an invisible life-force that permeates the universe and flows through all living things.

According to Tantrism, by getting close but not succumbing to orgasm during sex we can direct energy upward through specific points in the body called *chakras*. A prolonged state of sexual tension that isn't relieved by orgasm diverts energy from the base *chakra* (which is situated half-way between the anus and the genitals) upward. As the energy ascends through the *chakra*s, the Tantric student attains a progressively higher level of consciousness until finally, when energy reaches the highest *chakra* at the crown of the head, he or she experiences a state of pure being and oneness with the universe, free from the usual constraints of mind and ego.

The Tantric deferral of orgasm is called "riding the wave". The idea is that both partners move just enough to keep each other stimulated during sex, but not enough to push each other over the edge into orgasm. You can get a taste of what it's like to practise Tantric sex by trying the following meditation.

SENSUAL *CHAKRA* MEDITATION

First, you and your partner need to get into a relaxed mood. Share a bath together and spend some time talking and massaging each other. Do the sacral massage on pages 36–7.

When you feel prepared, sit in a cross-legged position facing each other and place your right hands over each other's heart –

imagine that sexual energy is flowing into you from your partner's body and vice versa. Breathe deeply and in time with each other. Gaze into each other's eyes.

The next step is to get into a sexual position in which the man stays sitting cross legged while his partner climbs onto his lap and wraps her legs around his waist. Then she gently guides his erect penis into her vagina.

Start by imagining a hotspot of sexual energy or tension concentrated in your perineum (your root *chakra*). Breathe in deeply together and imagine the energy rising into your abdomen (your spleen *chakra*) and fizzing and whirling inside you. The spleen *chakra* is the centre of sexual energy, so try to focus on erotic sensation. Inhale again and let the energy surge upward to the area just behind your navel (your solar-plexus *chakra*). On your next in-breath, feel energy flowing into your chest – this is your heart *chakra* and it governs your emotions, so concentrate on your innermost feelings of love for your partner. Now breathe in and take the energy from your chest into

your neck (the throat *chakra*). This *chakra* encourages self-expression. On your next two inhalations let the energy rise to the place between your eyes (your third-eye *chakra*) and, finally, the spot at the crown of your head (your crown *chakra*).

Throughout this meditation try to remain in a state of sexual arousal by rocking gently against one another. The woman can also contract her root lock (see pages 86–7) against the man's penis. If either of you feel as though you are going to climax, practice deep belly breathing (see pages 66–7).

YOGA-STYLE SEX

Practising yoga can be beneficial to sex in all sorts of ways. Some yoga poses tone the pelvic area, which can help to increase sexual sensation – the bow pose, in which you lie on your stomach and grab your ankles with your hands while lifting your thighs and chest off the floor, is one example. Yoga can make you generally supple and bendy so that you can have fun attempting all sorts of athletic sex positions. It also helps you to tune in to your body and concentrate on its responses. But perhaps the most useful are the specific yoga practices that can help to enhance orgasm.

CONTRACTING THE ROOT LOCK

In yoga, special techniques known as *bandhas* are used to lock energy (*prana*) into a particular part of the body. When it comes to sex, a special lock, known as the root lock, can intensify sexual sensation – and both men and women can practise it.

To practise contracting your root lock sit in a cross-legged position and pull up the muscles of your perineum – the muscles of

your anus and genitals will automatically contract as well. Now pull in the area beneath your navel. Imagine that you are trying to get your anus and navel to meet. Hold this contraction for as long as it is comfortable and then slowly release it. Repeat this five times, relaxing for 15 seconds in between each contraction. Do this once a day.

If you practise this regularly, the muscles surrounding your genitals will become very strong and your orgasmic contractions will feel more intense as a result. You can also flex your vaginal or penile muscles during sex and enhance sexual sensation this way. Some women with strong vaginal muscles can contract them in a fast, rhythmic flutter that feels great for both partners.

You can also practise this root-lock exercise while squatting – some people find they have a greater awareness of their pelvic muscles in this position. Squat down with your feet a little way apart and your toes pointing outward. Bring your elbows to the insides of your knees and put your hands together in a prayer position. Keep your feet flat on the floor – if this is difficult, put a folded blanket underneath your heels.

BELLY BREATHING WITH A DIFFERENCE

Belly breathing is a yoga technique in which you draw your breath deeply down into your lungs so that your diaphragm moves down and your abdomen swells (see exercise on pages 66–7). Once you can belly breathe with ease you can try another yoga technique which involves directing your breath to a specific part of your body, such as your genitals. Your breath doesn't actually get this far, but it's a way of sending energy to a particular body part and increasing sensation in that area.

To practise directional breathing, inhale deeply as usual but visualize the air being drawn down as far as your vagina or penis. Try to feel a warm, tingling or vibrating sensation in your genitals as you do this. When you've mastered this try practising it while you are having sex. Relish the pleasant sensations that flood into your genitals on each inhalation.

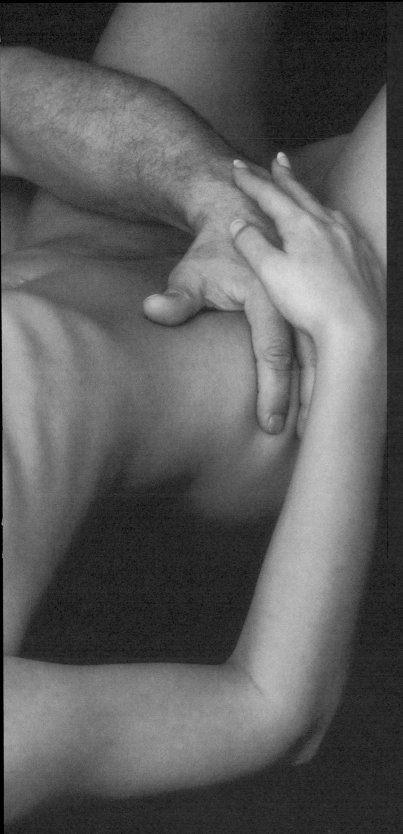

Sex is something that we tend to get on and do rather than sit down and think about. However, now that you are learning to explore new approaches to sex, it's time to reflect upon your own personal sexual style. Do you like the way you have sex? Do you ever feel in a rut? Do you communicate well with your partner about sex? Do you know how your unique sexual rhythms influence your libido? Do you understand why you are inhibited about some things and not about others? These are just some of the questions that I encourage you to think about in this chapter. Hopefully, the process of answering them will help to expand your sexual horizons.

5 REFLECTION

THE EROTIC JOURNAL

As part of a sex-therapy exercise, I once asked a woman to keep an account of her inner sex life, her dreams, her fantasies and her sexy thoughts. Although she claimed that she never experienced any of these things, by recording any erotic feelings she had she discovered that in fact one sexy thought leads to another …. It is a great shame that most of our sexual thoughts go unrecorded. Our dreams and fantasies give us the best and most interesting clues about what is going on in our unconscious mind and can lead us to greater self-knowledge.

WRITING IT DOWN

It's worth keeping a notebook beside your bed and logging any sexual dreams you have. They don't have to feature explicit sex scenes; they can simply be sensual or erotic in mood. You can also log your daytime thoughts and fantasies in your notebook.

Once you've got a few weeks' worth of entries read back over what you've written. Are there any consistent themes or patterns? How much does your inner sex life overlap with your actual sex life? Would you like this overlap to be bigger or smaller? As well as using your journal to explore your sexual unconscious, you can also use it as a source book to give you ideas about what you can do in bed with your partner. If there's a particular fantasy that you'd like to enact, my advice would be to read it aloud to your partner.

THE SEX JOURNAL

You can also keep a journal of your actual sexual life. This is an exercise that's good for couples who are having sexual problems because it allows them to take a cool, objective view of when and how they make love. To keep this kind of diary you need to log not just when you have sex but what you were doing beforehand and how you felt afterward. This quickly reveals negative sexual habits, such as making love after an argument or when you've been drinking, and how these things can lead to feelings of dissatisfaction. The build-up to sex and the circumstances in which you make love are important. Use your sex diary as a catalyst for change.

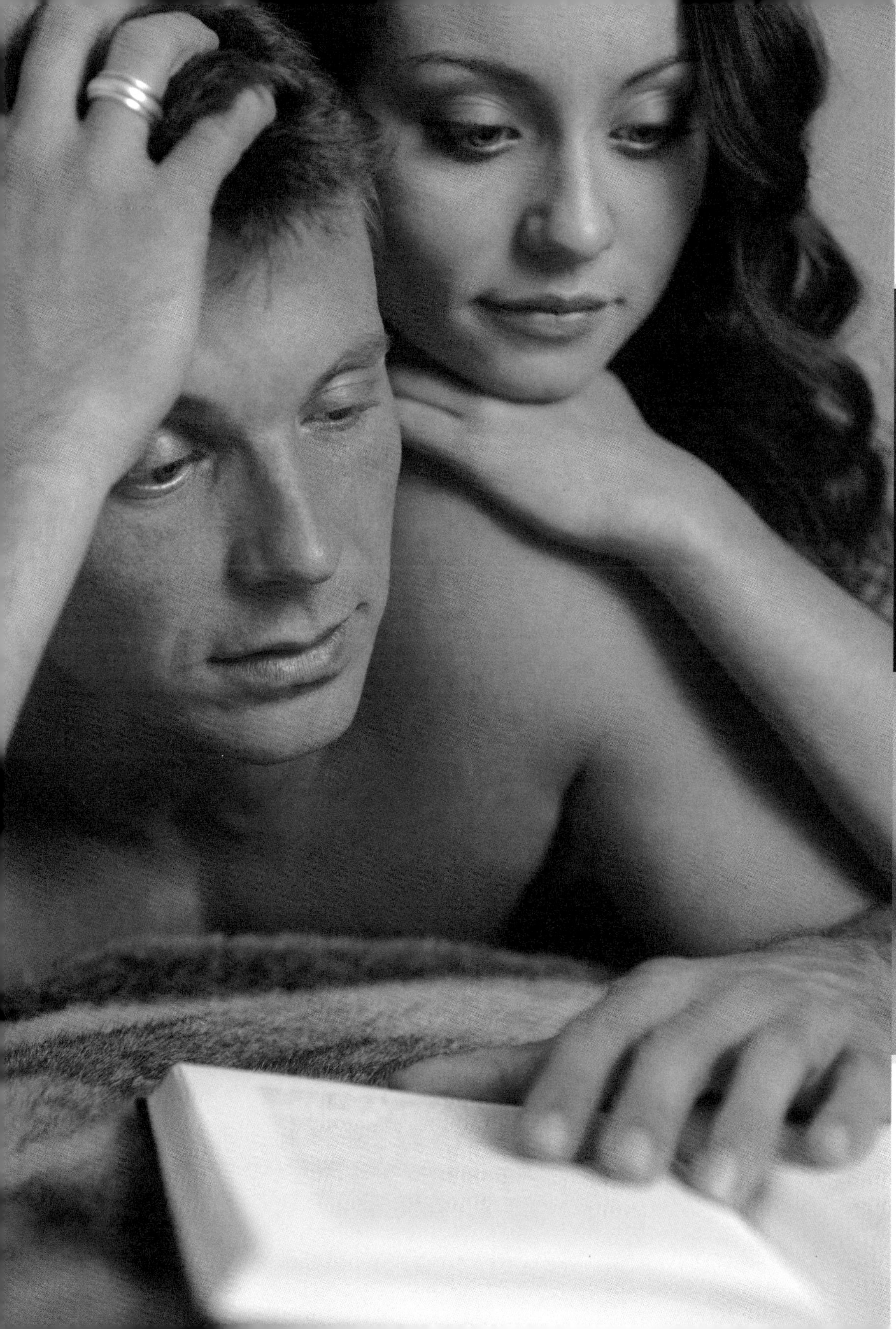

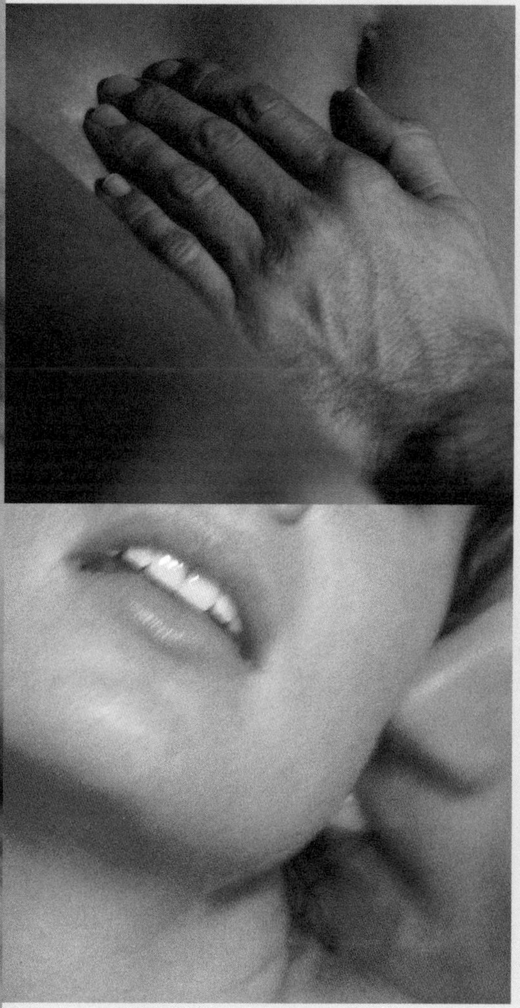

Creating a sexual timeline involves selecting the things in your life that you think have influenced you sexually and then plotting them chronologically on a line. This is a fascinating exercise that allows you to take an impartial look at your sex life up until now.

To begin with, draw a straight line across a large piece of paper. The left-hand end of this line represents your childhood and the right-hand end represents the present day. Now you need to plot your most significant sexual memories and experiences throughout your life along the timeline.

Each entry should describe the relevant sexual experience, your feelings about it at the time and the age you were when it happened. So, for example, an entry might read as follows: "Watched older brother kissing girlfriend; he was angry and told me to go away; age 6." Or: "Stranger tried to make a pass at me; felt scared/excited; age 15." Or: "Lost my virginity; felt relieved/nervous; age 17." Or: "Made love for the first time in more than a year; felt alive/sexy; age 45."

How detailed you make your timeline is entirely up to you. I suggest you restrict yourself to the events and experiences that have had a major emotional impact on you – the things that you will remember for the rest of your life. It's tempting to make your timeline more detailed as you begin to tackle your recent past, but try to resist doing this. Events that have happened in the last year or so may not turn out to be as influential in the long term as you imagine at the moment.

When you are satisfied that you have compiled a timeline that accurately depicts your sexual milestones, go back and mark each entry with a small arrow. An arrow that points upward represents an encounter that you feel positive about, while an arrow that points downward represents something that invokes negative feelings. If you're not sure how you feel about an event, draw a horizontal arrow.

It's easier to construct your timeline if you divide it into three parts: childhood memories, becoming sexually active and adult sexual experiences.

SEXUAL TIMELINE

CHILDHOOD MEMORIES

Start by thinking about your earliest memory of sex or sexual feelings. This could be anything from finding your parents making love to seeing someone naked, or exploring your genitals. Even if your early experiences seem odd, childish or inappropriate, include them.

Now brainstorm and think about your most influential sexual experiences after this. Here are some things to think about. How did your parents deal with the question "Where do babies come from?" Did you ever play "sexy" games at school such as kiss chase? Do you remember feeling curious about certain words, jokes or gestures? Were you ever told not to touch yourself "down there"? How did you learn about masturbation? Who told you about sexual intercourse and how? Did you ever wonder whether you were straight or gay? Can you remember your first crush?

BECOMING SEXUALLY ACTIVE

The next part of your sexual timeline (you might need to extend your line onto a new piece of paper at this point) consists of your most important experiences around the time when you became sexually active. Make a note of when you first masturbated/kissed someone/explored someone's body/made love and whether or not it lived up to your expectations. You can also include experiences that failed to happen – rejections and brush-offs or simply feelings of frustration that other people around you were becoming sexually active when you weren't. You can even include books and films that had a powerful sexual impact on you.

ADULT SEXUAL EXPERIENCES

Now add to the timeline brief descriptions of your most significant sexual encounters right up until the present day. Include the negative ones as well as the positive ones – it's often the negative experiences we have that we learn most from. Here are some questions to prompt you. When/how did your most important sexual relationships begin and end? What were the highs and the lows? Have you had any sexual experiences that were completely out of character for you? What have been your major regrets sexually? Have you ever pushed back the boundaries of your sex life and tried something new? If you have had children, how has this changed your sex life? Have you ever had an affair? Is there a particular conversation or event that has radically changed your mind about some aspect of sex?

READING YOUR TIMELINE

How you use your finished timeline is up to you. You might take the opportunity to reminisce and relive some happy sexual encounters. Or you could use the timeline therapeutically, to learn about yourself, uncover your sexual motivations and decide if there is anything that you would like to change or work upon.

Incidentally, a timeline is a useful thing to take along to a counsellor if you ever decide to embark on a course of sex or relationship therapy. A word of warning: if drawing your timeline unearths memories that you find too painful to deal with, please seek advice from a doctor, counsellor or sex therapist.

THE FOLLOWING QUESTIONS CAN HELP YOU TO INTERPRET YOUR TIMELINE:

- Do most of your arrows point up or down? How do you account for this?
- How would you sum up your early impressions of sex? If they were negative impressions have you managed to shake them off?
- Have your recent sexual experiences been consistently positive or negative? If so, why do you think that is?
- Do the same kinds of events keep repeating themselves in your timeline? If so, why do you think that is?
- If someone who didn't know you looked at your timeline how do you think they would describe you sexually?
- What emotions do you feel when you look at your timeline?

(This page) This is for fast, spontaneous sex when you don't have much time or space. She stands on tiptoes — or a step — and he penetrates her in a face-to-face standing position. It's best to be extremely aroused before you get into position as it's hard to sustain for a long time. She can facilitate penetration by wrapping one thigh around his waist. (Opposite) In this athletic position the woman takes the strain. He lies on his back while she straddles him with her back to him. She guides him inside her and then leans back to take her weight on her hands and feet. This gives her a foundation to raise and lower herself on his penis. He can use his hands to guide her or to caress her breasts.

SEX WITH THE SOUND ON

Many of us find sex very difficult to talk about on an intimate level. This is a great shame, because if couples can speak candidly about their needs and desires, this opens the gateway to a wonderfully intimate and passionate sex life.

FIND YOUR OWN STYLE

It's essential to find your own unique style for talking about sex. If "making love" sounds corny to you, use medical terms, sexual slang or a combination of the two. I know that there are some people who have trouble saying any words that are to do with sex; if this sounds like you, a helpful exercise is to make a list of the "worst-offending" words and to speak them aloud on your own in front of a mirror. You might feel silly, but this exercise really works.

When you come to talk to your partner about sex it helps if you've got some openers prepared. Here are some examples:

- "My favourite kind of sex is when ... "
- "Do you know what I fancy most about you?"
- "The one thing I'd love to try in bed is ... "
- "Do you want to hear a sexual fantasy?"

If you've got sexual problems that you want to talk about with your partner, there are sensitive techniques for broaching them (see pages 132–3).

TALKING DIRTY

Talking during sex is a matter of taste; it can make you cringe with embarrassment or ramp up your arousal levels. The only way to find out how you react is to experiment. Describe exactly what sexual acts you are going to perform on your partner and what you would like in return. You might start by saying something like, "I want you to stand perfectly still while I undress you and kiss your ... ." Choose words that you are comfortable with and, if you feel shy or inhibited, let humour come to your rescue – treat the exercise as a bit of a laugh.

You can also get into a relaxed mood with a glass of wine (alcohol is a great disinhibitor, although more than one or two glasses can play havoc with your sexual performance). And if you need inspiration, buy a book of erotica and read it aloud to your partner.

SEXUAL RHYTHMS

What makes you desire sex is a highly complex and individual matter. It can depend on everything from how you are getting on with your partner to how confident you feel about your body. But if you could strip away all the emotional and psychological factors to reveal what's behind the pure animal instinct to have sex you would probably be left with one thing: hormones.

Testosterone is the hormone that drives both men and women to have sex. The rise and fall of testosterone in a lifetime and even over the course of a month (in women) or a day (in men) can have an impact on your sex drive. Being aware of your own personal ebb and flow of testosterone – plus other hormones – means that you can choose the most rewarding times to make love.

THE MALE RHYTHM

It's a popular myth that men have flat hormone levels that remain the same from hour to hour, day to day and month to month. Although men don't experience the same dramatic peaks and troughs as women, men do have hormone cycles. For example, it's well established that testosterone levels are higher in the morning than at any other time of day. There is also evidence that mood and behaviour have an impact on testosterone levels. In a study of tennis players it was noted that winning at tennis was linked with a rise in testosterone while losing was linked with a decline.

Whether shifting levels of testosterone affect men's libido is a matter of debate, but it's worth observing your own sexual rhythms. For example, ask yourself at what time of the day or in what circumstances you are most likely to think about sex, initiate sex or masturbate. If things are going well for you or you enjoy some kind of success, does this make you desire sex? Jot these observations down in a diary to see if there is any discernible pattern.

THE FEMALE RHYTHM

The menstrual cycle is a finely tuned interplay of hormones. As each day of your cycle passes, your hormonal profile changes, and with it your mood and energy levels. One week you might

feel full of vigour and optimism and the next you might feel irritable and lethargic. The same goes for your libido: at some points in the menstrual cycle you may find it difficult to get aroused and you will have little genital sensitivity; at others your sex drive will be operating on a hair trigger and every touch will feel fantastic.

If you know how your body responds to hormones in the menstrual cycle, you can exploit this by foregoing sex during the low spells and concentrating on it during the high points.

There are three points in the menstrual cycle at which libido can peak – most women experience at least one of these peaks. The first possible peak is during the first part of your cycle during that "feel-good" oestrogen surge (oestrogen elevates mood and well-being); the second is ovulation, when testosterone hits its high point; and the third is immediately before or during menstruation.

Try charting your sexual rhythms on a menstrual calendar over a time span of at least three months. Draw a ring around the days when you feel sexy and see if you can detect a pattern. If you want a more detailed account, try keeping an erotic journal (see page 90).

ALTERNATIVE RHYTHMS

Not all women have periods. Women who are pregnant, breastfeeding, menopausal or post-menopausal have sexual rhythms that are still controlled by hormones but in a less "orderly" way than those of women who menstruate. Pregnancy turns some women off sex completely, while others learn to be multi-orgasmic for the first time. Similarly, breastfeeding mothers may have a healthy interest in sex or they may find that prolactin (the hormone that stimulates milk production) depresses libido. The menopause and post-menopause are also times when sex drive can go haywire. There is a growing trend to prescribe testosterone as part of a hormone-replacement therapy (HRT) package for middle-aged and older women – this is good news for women who find that lowered levels of natural testosterone reduce their sex drive. Anyone who has a permanently depressed libido should see a doctor.

Lots of couples have what I call "default sex". Rather than making an active choice about where, when and how they are going to make love, they do it in the way that presents the fewest challenges. This usually ends up being in the bedroom at the end of the day when they are tired.

My aim in this chapter is to show you some of the ways that you can extend the boundaries in your sex life, prevent boredom and keep sex exciting. This means debunking myths about what is and isn't acceptable during sex and opening yourself up to a range of possibilities, from erotica to vibrators.

6 EXPLORATION

PUSHING BACK THE BOUNDARIES

When you begin a new relationship with some one often you both go through an exhilarating, rollercoaster ride of sexual discovery. You try everything together, from making love on a park bench at midnight to covering each other in whipped cream and licking it off. You drop some of the old sexual habits that applied to your previous relationships and you learn a wealth of new ones.

SEXUAL TEMPLATES

Gradually, a few months into a relationship, you find a style and method of lovemaking that makes you both happy. It works for you, and so you stick to it. In time this approach solidifies into a kind of "sexual template".

Many couples' sexual templates can serve them well for years, but there almost always comes a time in a relationship when predictability can creep in. And this is danger-ous, not because it makes you sexually dysfunc-tional or incapable of enjoying sex, but because it dampens your enthusiasm for making love in the first place.

Like other aspects of your relationship, sex needs to stay dynamic. It needs to keep evolving to meet both your needs. This is why it's so important to keep pushing back the boundaries in your sex life.

I once encountered a couple who were very experimental in bed at the beginning of their relationship, but seven years on they made love only within strict parameters. Their reason for this was that, after being together for so long, they felt "too familiar" with one another. They described themselves as "more like siblings than lovers" and felt that it was somehow improper or embarrassing to make love in new or different ways. Neither of them dared to take the initiative in suggesting new ideas.

"THAT ISN'T ME"

The other thing that stops people pushing back sexual boundaries is what I refer to as the "that-isn't-me" argument. Rather than being open to all sexual possibilities, we tend to regard some things (for example, dressing up in erotic under-wear or using sex toys) as inconsistent with our self-image. The result: we often write off sexual activities that we haven't even tried.

NEW IDEAS

It's always possible to inject new life into your lovemaking, but it isn't necessarily easy to do so. It means identifying the areas where your sex life is static, exposing yourself emotionally to your partner and trying out new ways of relating to each other.

A common trend in long-term relationships is for sex to become deprioritized. If you want to shake up your sex life, try putting sex back at the top of your list of priorities. Allocate time for it, actively choose the venue for your lovemaking and think about ways in which you can be experimental.

The first step to expanding your sexual horizons is discussion: if you have been experimental in the past, talk about the things you used to do, what you enjoyed about them and why you stopped doing them. Ask your partner what new things he/she would enjoy in bed now and throw in plenty of ideas of your own.

SEX COMES NATURALLY

A very pervasive myth is that the ability to give sexual pleasure comes naturally and that good lovers have an innate sensual repertoire. An associated myth is that lovers should be mind readers – they should know how to please their partners without needing to ask questions or be given direction. This myth may help to explain why so many of us feel reticent about spelling out what we like during sex and asking detailed questions of our lovers.

EXPLODING THE MYTHS

People seem to internalize more myths about sex than almost any other subject. Some myths affect what you actually do in bed (for example, "sex isn't sex without penetration") while others affect how you feel about sex ("loving sex must be slow and tender"). Sometimes sexual myths are so insidious that we're not even aware of them.

MEN AND WOMEN HAVE DEFINED SEXUAL ROLES

This myth includes: men should always be able to get and keep an erection during sex; women should always have an orgasm – ideally from penetrative sex alone; men should make the first sexual advances; women must be young, slim and beautiful to be truly sexy; men must be sexually confident and capable even when they haven't had much experience; women must look (and sound) feminine during sex. And so on. Deep-rooted beliefs about gender are some of the hardest to shake off because they have often been instilled in us from childhood.

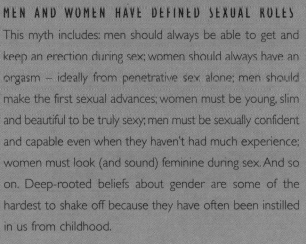

SOME TYPES OF SEX ARE WRONG OR DIRTY

It is important that sex has some boundaries. For example, sex should always be consensual and should never endanger physical or emotional health. But, beyond this, too many rules and limitations can take the fun out of sex and prevent you from expressing your sexual self to the full. For example, the idea that some types of sex – such as bondage, role-playing, watching erotic films or playing with sex toys – are in some way dirty, wrong or perverted may mean that you are cutting yourself off from a range of experiences that you might relish.

SEX WITH ONE PERSON GETS BORING

We are constantly sold the idea that we need variety and change in all aspects of our life. Yet we are expected to make love to one person for many months or years and, in the case of marriage, for a lifetime. The popular consensus is that sex eventually gets boring, and that desire gradually fades in long-term relationships. I think that this is a myth. If a relationship stays emotionally vibrant and dynamic and a couple is prepared to work at sex, then their relationship can stay erotic indefinitely.

YOUR OWN PERSONAL MYTHS

Try to uncover your personal myths about sex. You may buy into some of the myths described here or you may have your own completely idiosyncratic sexual mythology. Ask yourself which of your beliefs about sex are useful and which you need to reject because they are out-of-date, untruthful or prevent you from expressing your real self. Ask your partner what sexual myths he/she thinks you subscribe to and explore the subject together.

KISSING GAMES

No sexual act can compare in intensity to a passionate kiss. Kissing brings you into physical and emotional proximity in a way that no other lovemaking technique can match. One man told me that the most erotically charged moments of his entire life came when he knew that he was finally about to kiss the woman he had been in love with for more than two years.

Kissing is the body's way of saying "I want to be as close and connected to you as I possibly can." It transcends words and looks and is the most decisive statement of intimacy, desire and lust there can be.

This is why people who want to avoid intimacy and connection consciously or unconsciously neglect kissing. For example, most prostitutes draw the line at mouth-to-mouth contact. Couples in long-term relationships often just seem to "forget about" kissing even if they still make love on a regular basis. They may be good at perfunctory kissing on the lips, cheek or the top of the head, but this is no substitute for the intensity of a deep and soulful kiss that goes on for at least a minute.

HOT KISSING TIPS

New lovers are usually fiercely observant of the following rule while older, established lovers are prone to neglecting it: deep kissing is sexiest when each other's mouths taste scrupulously clean and fresh (and his skin is smooth and stubble-free). Try kissing each other after sucking a eucalyptus sweet, or cut a peach, pear or plum in half, feed each other and kiss the juice away.

There's something very sexy about being close to someone without actually touching them. Bring your face close to your lover's face so that your lips are just a hair's breadth apart. And now breathe softly. As he breathes out, you breathe in and so on. The feeling of each other's breath on the lips is extremely tantalizing. There's no doubt that this game will end in a kiss but you can up the erotic tempo by drawing it out as long as possible.

Some couples use kissing as a device to get them aroused before sex. As soon as they feel aroused they stop kissing and move on to the next stage of sex. If this describes you, try to forego sex one day and concentrate on

kissing instead – make it an end in itself instead of a means to an end.

Approach a kiss as you would the whole of sex. Start off softly and tentatively using just your lips, then make your kisses more energetic and urgent as you both become more turned on. Use your tongue and lips imaginatively – try gently sucking your partner's lower lip. One of the most intimate kissing games consists of breathing together. One of you takes a deep breath while the other exhales completely. Then make a seal between your lips and share the breath.

Save your most passionate kisses for the heady heights of intercourse when your tongue in her mouth echoes and emulates the penis inside the vagina.

Kissing doesn't have to be mouth-to-mouth. Try kissing and sucking each other's fingers, toes, earlobes, belly buttons and buttocks.

Finally, make kissing your preferred style of communication when you've been apart from each other. Don't bother with hello, just drop everything and close your eyes.

(This page) This is a variation of the missionary position in which the woman holds her thighs tightly together to create a snug fit for the man's penis. The higher the angle of penetration the greater the friction on the clitoris. Penetration can be deepened by placing pillows under the woman's hips. (Opposite) Commonly known as the "spoons position", this gentle, relaxing pose combines the excitement and deep penetration of rear-entry sex with comfort and emotional intimacy. His body moulds into the shape of hers and both partners can ease into sex because neither of them has to take any body weight — ideal during pregnancy or first thing in the morning.

LOVERS' PLAYTIME

Sex toys used to have a seedy reputation. However, they have recently come out of dingy, backstreet shops and are now available in respectable, high-street stores. There's no longer a stigma attached to owning a vibrator and it's widely accepted that toys can transform sex from a rather earnest, serious activity into something far more light-hearted and playful.

TOYS THAT GO BUZZ

The range of vibrators on the market is huge. They can be battery or mains operated, they can come with clitoral stimulators or G-spot attachments, they can be hard and metallic or soft and spongy. Some vibrators look exactly like penises, others are smooth and cylindrical and others are shaped like eggs. There are even some vibrators that look more like domestic appliances than sex toys.

To avoid being bewildered by the sheer diversity of products, it's best to decide in advance what you want from a vibrator. Many women say that the most reliable devices in terms of reaching orgasm are heavy-duty, mains operated vibrators that vibrate at a high intensity and don't run out at the critical moment. But if you want something discreet that you use only occasionally, choose a small, battery-operated vibrator. You also need to consider the noise factor: some people find noisy vibrators too loud and distracting to be sexy.

Use your vibrator imaginatively. Tease your lover with it. Vibrators aren't just for women, and they can be used on other parts of the body than the genitals – try a vibrator massage on the back, buttocks, thighs, breasts or even between the toes. Experiment with different speeds and pressures. If you are trying to have an orgasm with a vibrator, the trick is not to try too hard – just lie back and let the sensations build gradually. Try holding the vibrator so that the base touches the entrance to the vagina and the tip touches the clitoris or the glans of the penis – then gradually turn up the speed. A tip for men using vibrators on women: go for a "multiple-stimulation" approach to sex in which you use a vibrator and your fingers or penis at the same time.

STRAPS, CUFFS AND HARNESSES

Restraining toys, such as straps and cuffs, often conjure up forbidding images of black leather and hard-core S&M. This doesn't have to be the case: lots of restraining toys are made from fake fur and satin, with the emphasis on symbolic rather than actual restraint – think velcro rather than metal.

There is a wide range of restraining toys available, from hand and ankle cuffs to ropes, belts and tethers. Harnesses are used to attach a dildo to your body so that you can manipulate it against your partner without having to use your hands. Dildos are non-vibrating penis substitutes (by the way, if you want to experiment with anal insertion make sure you choose a dildo that has a flared end, which prevents it from slipping inside completely).

PADDLES, WHIPS AND CLAMPS

Only a tiny minority of lovers are seriously turned on by inflicting or receiving pain during sex, and for many people S&M toys have an intimidating reputation. However, the new

generation of these toys are playful rather than menacing. In fact, they're more likely to be called "sensation toys" than S&M toys. Examples include whips made from strands of purple suede, pink feather dusters, fur-lined paddles for spanking and lightweight, vibrating nipple clamps.

Use toys like these to experiment with new skin sensations. Take turns with your partner to be the "victim" (but first establish a code word to alert him or her if you want them to stop). The combination of novel physical sensation and psychological domination can be a heady mixture in lighthearted S&M games.

ANAL TOYS

The anus is an area that is rich in nerve endings and exquisitely sensitive. If you like being touched in this area you can expand your sexual repertoire by using anal toys. There are three basic types: plugs that are inserted into the rectum but are prevented from slipping inside by a flared base, anal vibrators (also with a flared base) and anal beads – a string of small, medium or large beads attached to a ring and designed to be inserted into the rectum and slowly pulled out again.

If you experiment with anal toys always follow these rules:

• Use plenty of lubrication – unlike the vagina, the anus and rectum are not self-lubricating.

- Always focus on relaxing the anal muscles during anal play – never force anything into the anus.
- Don't use an anal toy in the vagina without sterilizing it first.

JUST FOR MEN

The most common sex toys available for men are penis rings and pumps. The penis ring locks blood into the penis, maintaining a firm erection.

However, some penis rings are purely decorative or have protruding clitoral attachments that are designed to stimulate a female partner. Penis rings can be made out of rubber, metal, leather or plastic – some of them even vibrate. Penis pumps consist of tubes that are placed around the penis – as the air is pumped out of the tube a vacuum forms around the penis causing blood to rush into the shaft, creating a strong erection. Men with erectile difficulties

(see pages 144–5) may use penis pumps to enable them to have sex, but lots of other men use them simply to produce a larger and harder erection than they would have ordinarily.

Whether penis rings and pumps make a difference to sexual sensation for either partner is up to you to decide. What they can do is allow women to focus attention on their partner's genitals, something which both parties can enjoy.

SENSORY DEPRIVATION

Good sex relies on all five of our senses: the touch of one body against another; the unique smell and taste of a lover's skin; the vocal sounds of desire; and the sight of the curves, textures and angles of the human body. All these things contribute to a complete sensual and erotic experience.

However, it's interesting to play around with the senses. For example, what happens if you take away someone's sight by blindfolding them? What happens if you restrict someone's freedom to touch by binding their wrists with light restraints? What happens in the most extreme form of sensory deprivation, in which you take away touch, smell, taste and sight and have to make love to someone with words alone (see page 99)? I think these kinds of deprivation can be positive in that they help us to become more imaginative, creative and exploratory lovers.

If you choose to experiment with sensory deprivation you'll find that your other senses become magnified. The blindfolded person develops a heightened awareness of sound;

the handcuffed person becomes greedy for touch; lovers who are physically apart are forced to the limits of their linguistic powers.

PERMISSION TO BE HELPLESS

If you haven't got a proper blindfold, improvise with some fabric or a scarf or even a pair of panties. As soon as one of you puts on a blindfold you will slip into passive and dominant roles. If you are the "blind" partner you will be reduced to a state of vulnerability and anticipation. This can be a great thing for men who tend to play the dominant role during sex and need special "permission" to lie back and feel helpless. Another benefit of sight deprivation is that your mind is undistracted by the usual visual stimuli and is allowed to come up with spontaneous erotic images of its own.

If you are the "sighted" partner you can play around with feelings of sexual power – this can be particularly liberating if you usually feel shy or self-conscious in bed. You can lead the sexual encounter in any direction you like – by giving or demanding long, slow oral sex or by

trying out a variety of sexual positions on your partner. You can also exploit your partner's suggestibility by planting images in his or her head. You can be the headmaster, she can be the schoolgirl or she can be the doctor, you can be the patient. You can also "invent" the room that you are in – for example, a harem or an S&M den. Make your role-plays as lavish as you like.

RESTRAINING YOUR PARTNER

Tying up your partner with soft cords, scarves or stockings can create the same sort of passive-versus-powerful relationships as blindfolding can (in fact, you can combine the two). The tied partner can be kept in a state of extreme erotic suspense while the dominant partner gets to do all the things that really turn him or her on. Tie your partner's wrists and ankles to the bed but keep the ties loose – the restraint really only needs to be symbolic. On the other hand, if you do go for more serious bondage games, make sure that you have a code word that means "stop" (lovers often shout "stop" at the height of passion and actually mean the opposite).

SEX ONLINE

The arrival of the world-wide web has changed sex for ever. It's now possible to register at an online-dating website and be corresponding with potential partners within minutes. If you hit it off with someone – geography permitting – you could be on a date with them within the hour. Alternatively, if you fancy chatting to someone anonymously, you can log on to a sex chatroom, invent an exotic sexual persona for yourself and be talking – or writing – dirty in the time that it would normally take you to undress. Or, for vast numbers of people, sex on the Internet means the ability to download a diverse and explicit array of pornography in a matter of seconds.

THE POWER OF THE WWW

The Internet has the power for both good and bad. On the negative side, it can make love, sex and relationships feel impersonal, cheap, superficial or depressing – ultimately, nothing can replace the warmth, passion and intimacy of real-life sex with someone you truly desire. However, on the positive side, the Internet can help to break down sexual boundaries in new and unpredictable ways. Issues such as beauty, body shape and even gender and race are rendered irrelevant by the anonymity of the Internet.

An ever-increasing number of people around the world are learning to flirt electronically, without the usual inhibitions that can so often hamper face-to-face communication. It's much less risky, on an emotional level, to reveal your true feelings via email than it is in the flesh. A fast exchange of emotionally charged emails often results in relationships becoming intimate and intense very quickly. Sometimes, it's possible for you to feel that you know or love someone before you have even met them.

COUPLES ONLINE

It is often said that sex on the Internet is for single people rather than for couples. Most online pornography is used by single men, and the majority of people who use chatrooms and dating websites tend also to be single.

However, I believe that couples can also exploit the Internet for the good things it can offer. Here are some ideas:

• The Internet contains plenty of soft porn and erotica that can be enjoyed by couples. If you're open-minded, trawl through some sex sites with your partner. The more you narrow down your search to match your specific tastes the better. For example, searching for "erotic fiction" or "*Kama Sutra* sex positions" should screen out most hard-core pornography. Talk about what you like and what you find distasteful with your partner and treat your surfing as a voyage of discovery.

• Go sex shopping on the Internet together. People who feel reticent about stepping through the door of a sex shop may feel perfectly at home in the virtual equivalent – especially women. Buy some sex toys or erotica from a good-quality website.

• Introduce an electronic side to your relationship. Use emails to flirt, be suggestive or to say the things that you feel shy about when you are face-to-face with your partner.

FANTASY LIFE

There used to be something shameful about sexual fantasies. People who needed them were perceived as single, solitary masturbators who couldn't get their hands on a real-life partner. Or, if you had a partner and still needed fantasies, you obviously didn't fancy him or her enough. A fantasy was considered an inferior and artificial way of boosting arousal.

Fortunately, attitudes have changed considerably. During the sexual revolution of the 1960s and 1970s, sexual fantasies came out of the closet and were dusted off and examined afresh. Instead of being a sad sexual crutch, a fantasy came to be seen as a valid form of sexual expression.

Writers and sex researchers such as Shere Hite and Nancy Friday have found that most people have sexual fantasies and that, instead of being dysfunctional, this is completely normal. Nancy Friday, whose collections of male and female fantasies have been reprinted dozens of times since the 1970s and 1980s, describes fantasies perfectly as "the true X-rays of our sexual souls".

WHAT IS A FANTASY?

A sexual fantasy is anything you want it to be. It can be a fleeting mental image of your ideal lover or it can be a detailed erotic story with a convoluted plot. Fantasies range from the relatively mundane — recalling a previous episode of lovemaking with your partner — to the wild: for example, kinky sex with a group of strangers in a rapidly ascending lift.

You need only to look at *Women on Top* (1992) or *Men in Love* (1980), both by Nancy Friday, to discover the great diversity of sexual fantasies that both sexes enjoy.

THE ROLE OF FANTASY

Fantasizing is a way of becoming mindful during sex. It enables you to immerse yourself in the moment and be free of other preoccupations. A compelling fantasy can lift an ordinary sexual experience into the realm of the extraordinary. The reason that fantasies are so powerful is that they come directly from the unconscious mind — the place where all of our most deeply rooted and primitive feelings about sex reside.

Sex therapists often "prescribe" fantasy homework to clients who are experiencing sexual difficulties, such as problems reaching orgasm or getting an erection. Fantasies can give you that extra "nudge" that allows you to overcome sexual blocks or inhibitions and truly learn how to let go.

Of course, how you use fantasy is up to you. You can add spice and variety to your sex life with your partner by discussing some of your fantasies openly with each other. You can also use fantasy to achieve fast and intense orgasms when you masturbate on your own. Some women rely on fantasy to enable them to catch up with a partner who gets aroused much more quickly than they do.

YOUR INNER SEX LIFE

No one can tell you what to fantasize about because everyone has their own unique set of erotic triggers. However, I can tell you how to fantasize freely. Although we're all much more liberated about sexual fantasies than we were 20 or 30 years ago, I often hear people say that they still feel guilty about fantasizing. I think the reason for this is that sexual fantasies, by definition, contain erotically sensitive material – perhaps the kind of thing you wouldn't necessarily want to confess to your partner. It's often those things that we consider dirty, naughty or taboo that really turn us on. In fact, we frequently fantasize about acts that we would never want to happen in real life: sex with someone of our own gender; orgies; or even sex that involves force. But perhaps the most potentially offensive fantasy is also the most common: sex with someone other than our current partner.

I think the answer to the problem of guilt is simply to live with it. You could even argue that fantasies would lose their power if they were stripped of the ability to shock or offend. If you feel guilty about fantasizing, remind yourself that everyone is entitled to an inner sex life as well as a "real life" one. It's only when fantasies threaten to take over your thoughts or have a negative impact on your relationship that you need to worry.

USING EROTICA

Do pornography and erotica have a role to play in a healthy sex life? This is a contentious question that often rears its head in relationships. Some people are at ease with porn and see it as harmless. Others see porn as exploitative and degrading to both the people who make it and those who use it.

One of the problems inherent in porn is that, traditionally, it has been created by men for men. As a result, it tends to centre around popular male fantasies about women and sex – or at least what the creators of porn believe to be popular male fantasies. For example, the main protagonists in porn movies tend to be young, thin, large-breasted women who have insatiable sexual appetites. The inevitable result is that lots of women feel excluded or alienated by pornography and men regard it as a solitary habit that it's not appropriate to share.

RECLAIMING PORN

One solution to this is to try to rescue pornography from an exclusively male viewpoint. I think that it can be perfectly natural and healthy to feel aroused by the sight of others making love – as long as both genders can relate to the people involved and sex is portrayed with warmth and emotion. Fortunately, there is a growing amount of pornography – some of which is created by women – that is made from a more rounded perspective and which aims to depict both male and female sexuality in an authentic way. Or you can follow the example of one couple I know who, dissatisfied with the range of erotic material available, decided to create their own pornography – for private viewing only of course.

PORNOGRAPHY VERSUS EROTICA

There is a fine line between porn and erotica, but the main distinction is that erotica is deemed to have some artistic or literary merit, whereas pornography sets out solely to titillate its audience. If you find the idea of pornography offensive, there is a wide range of beautiful erotic art from countries such as China, Egypt, India and Greece. Try looking at some of the illustrations from Chinese pillow books.

TESTING YOUR BOUNDARIES

Despite the fact that, for many people, porn has negative associations, it does have its advantages. It can boost your desire for sex and raise your arousal levels if they are flagging. If you choose material carefully, porn can be fun, entertaining and inspiring. It can help to reduce inhibitions and give you new ideas to try out in bed. Also, if you feel reticent about talking to your partner in detail about sex, porn can kick-start a conversation and help you to be more candid.

If you want to try looking at porn with your partner, browse the Internet using carefully selected search criteria (see page 121) or watch a film such as *Ai No Corrida* (In the Realm of the Senses) or *9½ Weeks*. Work out where your tastes overlap and where they differ. Ask each other:

• If you had taken this picture or directed this film (for example) what do you think you would you have done differently?

• What specifically turns you on about this?

• What specifically offends you about this?

• Does looking at porn/erotica get you in the mood for sex more quickly or make you more aroused?

• What other differences – good and bad – does porn/erotica make to sex?

• How often should porn/erotica be part of our sex life?

You need to be aware that, as with anything that is used to excess, pornography and erotica have the potential to damage as well as enhance your sex life. For example, excessive use of pornography may lead to an inability to do without it. The danger signs of pornography dependence are feeling bored by or indifferent to sex that doesn't involve porn or being unable to get properly aroused in the absence of porn.

Another danger inherent in pornography is jealousy. I know of one man who became jealous that his wife was more turned on by lesbian erotica than she was by him. If you are worried about this becoming an issue for you, talk about it with your partner before it threatens to damage your sex life.

Most of us find sex problems difficult to admit to. We would prefer to struggle on, having unfulfilling sex, rather than face the possibility that this most private part of our lives isn't working. Often it's only when sex problems spill over into the rest of the relationship, and one partner has an affair or threatens to leave, that we are galvanized into action. But by then it may be too late. My advice is to tackle sex problems head on. It's difficult but, ultimately, it can save your relationship. In this chapter I discuss the most effective self-help measures for sexual problems – all of them are tried and tested and come from years of practical experience of counselling and sex therapy.

7 TROUBLE-SHOOTING

DIY SEX THERAPY

In the 1970s a psychologist called Jack Annon devised an approach to sex problems that could be applied to everything from premature ejaculation to sexual shyness. He named this new approach PLISSIT. Although PLISSIT was originally designed to be used by professionals such as doctors and therapists, it can also be adapted for use at home by people who want to try sexual self-help.

PLISSIT is an acronym. The letters stand for the following: P = Permission granting; LI = Limited Information; SS = Specific Suggestions; IT = Intensive Therapy. Here's how you can use PLISSIT at home.

GIVING YOURSELF PERMISSION

People who have sexual anxieties or problems often simply need reassurance that what they need or want sexually is normal and acceptable rather than wrong, dirty or weird. For example, a woman who doesn't reach orgasm from intercourse alone might need reassurance that it is completely normal to require extra manual stimulation. Or a man might need reassurance

that it's sometimes OK to say no to sex; that his sexual prowess doesn't depend on having a permanently switched on libido.

Being granted permission to feel or behave in a certain way can often solve sexual anxieties without the need for any further action. I know of one woman who thought she was a sexual failure for only ever being able to have one orgasm (as opposed to multiple orgasms). When she learned that this was perfectly normal she relaxed about her sex life and her feelings of self-criticism evaporated. If you find giving yourself permission to be sexual in a certain way is difficult ask yourself the following questions.

If you were to express yourself sexually in the way that you want to, would it:

- hurt you physically or emotionally?
- hurt anyone else physically or emotionally?
- make you afraid that your partner wouldn't like/love or respect you any more?
- push out the boundaries of how you think of yourself sexually?

If you answer "yes" to the first two options, then there are probably good reasons for not expressing yourself in your chosen sexual style. If, on the other hand, you answer "yes" to the last two options then you're probably acting out of fear and it may be time to challenge your assumptions and values about sex. Try to find out how your sexual attitudes originated (see pages 92–5) and ask yourself whether they are old, out-of-date or based on myth (see pages 108–109). Try to challenge what you think you "know" about sex. Be generous with yourself – allow your sexual barriers to come down and try to suspend that self-critical voice.

INFORMING YOURSELF

The "limited information" stage of Jack Annon's PLISSIT approach is about education. Many sex problems start because you are lacking some crucial piece of information. By filling in the information gap you can often solve the problem. An example might be a post-menopausal woman who doesn't know that her changed hormone levels can result in vaginal dryness, which, in turn, can make intercourse uncomfortable. Once she understands this she can

take action by using a lubricating jelly, by taking HRT or by slowing things down during sex to give her body chance to "catch up".

If you feel anxious about an aspect of your sex life, attempt to find out about it. Read about it, ask friends (they may have had similar experiences) and consult professionals. If you have concerns of a medical nature – for example, whether to have sex after a heart attack or a hysterectomy – ask your doctor to advise you or to recommend a source of information.

SPECIFIC ACTIONS

The next step of PLISSIT is to follow a program that is designed to help resolve your particular sex problem. The sex detox, which I have written about on pages 50–53, is an excellent way of letting go of all your habitual and problematic ways of making love. It can help to overcome a huge range of sex problems, from low sex drive to problems reaching orgasm. Try it. I have also outlined self-help treatment programs for premature ejaculation (see pages 138–9), erectile difficulties (see pages 144–5),

problems reaching orgasm during intercourse (see pages 70–73) and disagreements between couples about what types of sex they need or want (see pages 134–5).

INTENSIVE THERAPY

The final stage of PLISSIT, "intensive therapy", sounds daunting, but it doesn't have to be. It simply refers to the next stage of problem solving, which is seeking the advice of a professional. If none of the previous suggestions has helped you, the chances are that you would benefit from treatment by a doctor, pyschotherapist, relationship counsellor or sex therapist. If you have a problem that you suspect may have a physical origin (for example, difficulty getting or keeping an erection), then your first port of call should always be your doctor. If, on the other hand, you know that your problems are emotional or resulting from the relationship you are in, it is a good idea to contact a local or national association for sexual and relationship therapy, which should be able to refer you to an appropriate therapist.

DIY COUNSELLING

Most emotional and sexual problems can be resolved by talking. By this, I mean talking impartially and fairly without blaming, arguing, criticising or lecturing. This can be difficult when you're feeling upset and anxious. Sometimes professional counselling is the best way forward, but the following techniques, which are borrowed from counselling, can help you to talk constructively together at home as a couple.

BROACHING A PROBLEM

Pick a good time to talk – a time when there are no distractions and both of you are in a relatively calm mood and have guaranteed privacy. Invite your partner to sit down with you, and be specific about what you want to talk about. Know what you want to say, how you are going to say it and know what you hope to achieve. And make a commitment to listen fully to what your partner has to say. All too often, conversations between couples spiral out of control because one or both partners fail to listen properly. Another common problem is that people draw in all sorts of issues or grievances that are years old and have only a tenuous bearing on the current discussion.

HOW TO CRITICIZE

Criticism invariably makes us feel upset and undermined and immediately puts us on the defensive. This is why, if you feel critical of your partner, a good tip is to turn your complaints into suggestions or requests. For example, instead of saying, "I hate the fact that you never show me any affection any more", you might say, "I love it when you kiss me gently on the lips and put your arms around me." This way, instead of feeling attacked, your partner gets some honest guidance about what you really need and want.

Psychologists recommend speaking in a way that shows you are taking responsibility for your feelings rather than blaming them on others. Statements that begin with words such as: "You upset me when you ... " sound blaming and critical. Statements that begin with: "I feel upset when ... " sound more impartial and suggest that the speaker "owns" his or her feelings.

Try to mix constructive criticism with compliments. We all need to be reminded of the good things about ourselves, and if we feel confident that we are doing some things well we are more open to the possibility of changing other areas of our lives. Three tips for paying compliments: be as generous as possible; be specific; and always couch your compliments in the first person. For example, say, "I love the way you massage me", rather than "you're good at massage". People absolutely thrive on this kind of praise.

THE BROKEN-RECORD TECHNIQUE

Sometimes discussions can hit an impasse because one person is vague or reticent or quite simply refuses to budge on an issue. In this situation, counsellors recommend the "broken-record" technique. It involves repeating the same thing in a variety of different ways until the conversation starts to move forward again. The keys to this technique are to stay focused on the subject (ignore any tangential issues that your partner brings up) and to remain absolutely calm and speak in a neutral tone of voice. So, for example, you might say, "You haven't initiated sex much recently and I wondered if you wanted to talk about it", followed by, "Can we talk about our sex life? You don't seem to want to make love as often as you used to." And so on.

THE MIRRORING EXERCISE

This is one of the most valuable yet simple techniques in counselling. It involves paraphrasing what your partner has just said to you and then asking for confirmation that you've made a correct summary. The great thing about mirroring is that it removes all ambiguity from communication and makes you really tune in to what your partner is saying (as opposed to what you would like him or her to say). The first time you try mirroring it will probably feel like a very time-consuming way to communicate, but it does yield results fast. You quickly come to understand your partner's perspective and, because you are busy summarizing each other, it keeps you calm and prevents arguments from developing.

I've come across couples who talk over a sex problem and eventually, through negotiation and compromise, decide upon a new direction in their sex life. But as time passes, their plans go astray and the original sex problem lingers on. This is where the sex contract comes in. A sex contract is a written commitment by both partners to make specific changes to the way they make love. It is a sexual "to do" list.

Some people react negatively to the idea of a written contract when it comes to sex because they believe that sex should be natural, spontaneous and impossible to pin down with words. I would argue that a sex contract doesn't take the fun or the magic out of sex; instead it creates a framework for you to have better sex on a more equal footing with your partner.

HOW TO MAKE A SEX CONTRACT

The sex contract should start by couching the problem as a request. For example, if one partner never initiates sex, this could be phrased as: "R wants H to initiate lovemaking at least once a fortnight." Making precise requests enables you to monitor whether or not change is actually happening.

Next outline your plan. Be as specific as possible. If, for example, one partner doesn't receive enough foreplay to feel properly aroused, he/she needs to define exactly what they want. Is stroking each other's bodies a turn-on? What about oral sex? The more detail the better. For example: "I love having my breasts touched until I'm really turned on" or "I enjoy oral sex immediately before we have intercourse." This level of detail may feel clinical, but it will definitely change the way you make love because it eliminates ambiguity. When you're confident that the original sex problem has gone away you can be less formulaic.

It's important that both partners share the responsibility for a sexual problem. A sex contract shouldn't just be a list of requests drawn up by the partner who is dissatisfied. Work together to come up with suggestions and ideas and make sure that you are both happy with everything – your contract won't work if one of you disagrees with it.

THE SEX CONTRACT

When you have differences in sexual tastes. For example, where one partner likes S&M and the other doesn't. In this case, your sex contract should include a list of activities that the "reluctant" partner simply cannot tolerate. Spell out any caveats to this if appropriate. For example, "I don't like any S&M gear, but I don't mind having my wrists tied with a scarf." Now write a list of activities that you are willing to consider sometimes (pin down a time scale: once a week?), and, finally, those activities that you are most comfortable with. As long as your partner agrees with your lists, you now have a clear set of boundaries to proceed with in your sex life.

WHEN A SEX CONTRACT IS USEFUL

A sex contract can help to solve a wide range of sexual problems. The following are just examples — with a little imagination, it's possible to tailor the sex contract to help with almost any problem. The contract is especially useful if you don't want to spend a long time analyzing the roots of a sexual problem: the focus is on action rather than reflection.

When there are differences in your sexual appetites. For example, when one partner wants sex a lot more frequently than the other. In this case, the sex contract should allocate three days of the week to one partner and three days to the other (alternatively, each partner can be allocated alternate weeks). Each partner is allowed to veto or request sex on the days that belong to them. The decision about whether or not to have sex on the remaining day of the week should be mutual.

When the problem is one of sexual boredom. For example, where one or both partners lack the incentive to make love. In this case, the sex contract should include a list of activities aimed at trying to reinvigorate lovemaking. These should be mutually agreed. The contract should also specify the times that you can dedicate to lovemaking. If your chosen activities need some advance preparation, such as buying sex toys or renting a video, use the contract to specify who should do what.

THE REVIEW

After a few weeks of following the ideas in your sex contract, set a time with your partner for a review. Has your lovemaking changed for the better? Is there anything in the contract that needs to be added to, changed or made more specific? Take turns to say how you both feel and then make a joint decision about how your sex life should progress from now on.

When the couple has problems relating to sexual power. The sex contract should describe the things that are responsible for the dominated partner feeling the way he/she does. This might include always being made love to from behind (in the case of a woman) or being told what to do in bed. Beside each complaint write a suggestion for an alternative way of making love. For example, you might write: "I'd like to choose the sex position every other time we make love" or "I'd like us to have a break during sex when I say the words 'slow down'." The dominant partner should also contribute suggestions for a gentler way of making love.

TAKING CONTROL

How long should a man last in bed? This is one of those questions that's impossible to answer and one that lots of men get hung up upon. Some couples find three-minute intercourse satisfying; others don't feel content with anything less than 30 minutes. I've met lots of women who say that they would prefer 10 minutes of really skilled foreplay to 20 minutes of thrusting. Yet many men believe that they cannot be good lovers unless they are able to power away for an indefinite length of time, and they feel very anxious if they think they ejaculate too quickly to satisfy their partner.

Part of the problem is that, whereas men want to make love in a slow, considered way, they often masturbate themselves to orgasm very quickly – sometimes in seconds. Some men – particularly those who are young and sexually inexperienced – have trained themselves to climax so quickly that they find it hard to slow down their ejaculatory responses in order to meet the needs of a partner.

Ultimately, sexual staying power is a subjective issue and one that only you and your partner can resolve. Having said this, there are some men who operate on a hair trigger when it comes to ejaculation, and this can be extremely frustrating for both partners. If you ejaculate after minimal sexual contact (for example, if your penis is touched briefly) or very shortly after penetration then you can improve your sexual satisfaction greatly by learning ejaculatory control.

THE STOP/START TECHNIQUE

This is the time-honoured sex-therapy technique for treating premature ejaculation and it really does work. It teaches you to be confident about recognizing your ejaculatory responses and drawing back from them when you need to. It consists of the following six steps:

- Step 1: The woman stimulates the man's erect penis with her hand until he feels that he is about to ejaculate, at which point he tells her to stop.
- Step 2: The woman stops stimulation for between one and two minutes, during which time the man's arousal levels should fall.

- Step 3: The woman repeats this stop/start technique a total of four times. On the fifth time she continues to stimulate the man's penis until he ejaculates.
- Step 4: When the man becomes adept at controlling his ejaculation using the stop/start technique (usually over a period of weeks) the woman should make stimulation more sensual by coating her hand in massage oil. This mimics the feeling of the penis inside the vagina and feels much more erotic than dry masturbation.
- Step 5: Now it's time to have penetrative sex using the "quiet vagina" technique. The woman sits astride the man and guides his penis into her vagina. Both partners remain perfectly still. This enables the man to monitor and control his ejaculation in an erotic situation. If the man feels he is about to ejaculate, the woman should move off him.
- Step 6: The final stage of the stop/start technique involves having "normal" intercourse, during which the man thrusts inside the woman's vagina. By now most men have gained so much confidence about ejaculatory timing that they can sustain an erection for longer during sex.

THE SQUEEZE TECHNIQUE

This is another way of controlling ejaculation – it's a kind of "on-the-spot" treatment, so, unlike the stop/start technique, you don't have to do lots of practice before you see results. You can also use the squeeze technique in conjunction with the stop/start technique.

When you begin to feel you are close to ejaculating, simply withdraw (if you are having intercourse) and squeeze the head of the penis – put your first two fingers on the underside of the glans and your thumb on the top of the penis (your partner can do this just as well). Alternatively, you can squeeze at the base of the penis – this means you don't have to withdraw if you are in the middle of intercourse. Wherever you squeeze, apply pressure for 15 to 20 seconds. This should be enough to inhibit the ejaculatory reflex and enable you to carry on making love.

One of the most common sexual problems women experience is difficulty reaching orgasm during intercourse. Personally, I think that this is so widespread (only a minority of women climax without additional clitoral stimulation) that it shouldn't even be thought of as a problem.

The reason that the female orgasm is elusive during intercourse is the position of the clitoris; because it is situated a few centimetres away from the vagina it receives very little friction from the thrusting penis, and the friction that it does receive is indirect and sporadic. The result is that it doesn't matter how aroused the woman feels, she doesn't get the fast, direct and ongoing stimulation she needs to have an orgasm.

Lots of couples get over this problem by stimulating the clitoris with a vibrator or by hand during sex (the hand can be the man's, the woman's or both can be used). Or she can have an orgasm before or after intercourse. The other alternative is that you experiment with various sexual positions to find out whether there's one that provides an extra bit of stimulation in the right place for you.

THE CAT SOLUTION

CAT stands for Coital Alignment Technique and it was "invented" by Edward Eichel in the 1990s. The idea behind CAT is that the man penetrates his partner in the missionary position at a much higher angle than usual. This makes it possible for the penis to thrust directly against the clitoris.

In order to try CAT, the woman should lie on her back with her legs apart. After the man has entered her, he should shift his entire body weight up along her body (this may not seem like a very big movement) so that his pelvis is slightly higher than hers. She should then wrap her legs around his and rest her feet on his calves. Now when he moves, the clitoris should be directly stimulated by the base of his penis. For even better results, try combining CAT with the following movement.

BUMPING AND GRINDING

Most men thrust in and out of their partner's vagina during intercourse, but an alternative technique — and one that can help some

SPECIAL POSITIONS FOR WOMEN

women to be orgasmic – is a bumping, rocking or side-to-side grinding motion that exposes the clitoris to lots of friction.

Women can do the grinding themselves if they sit on top of the man – the best position is for her to put her knees on either side of her partner's waist and then rock backwards and forwards or, alternatively, make circular movements with her pelvis.

SIDE-BY-SIDE

Whether side-by-side sex positions work for you depends largely on your and your partner's anatomy. The following position can help some women to become orgasmic, particularly when the man has a large penis.

Both partners should lie on their sides facing each other. The woman lifts her upper thigh over the man's waist. He then puts his upper thigh across her lower one (which results in a kind of scissors arrangement) and penetrates her. With any luck, as he starts thrusting, the base of his penis will move in a rubbing motion across her clitoris.

PERFORMANCE PROBLEMS

Being unable to get or keep an erection is one of the sex problems that men find most upsetting. It cuts to the heart of male identity and the beliefs that lots of men – and women, for that matter – hold about sexual prowess and competence. For many men impotence – or erectile dysfunction, to give it its proper medical name – signals a hurtful loss of masculinity and a humiliating sexual defeat.

Every man encounters occasional erection problems – perhaps you've drunk too much alcohol, are too sleepy for sex or feel so distracted or preoccupied by a problem in another area of your life that you can't concentrate on feeling properly aroused. However, it's when your sex life becomes dogged with repeated performance problems that you really need to take action.

THE RIGHT DIAGNOSIS

Obtaining an accurate diagnosis is of absolutely critical importance when it comes to erection difficulties. There are several illnesses, including diabetes and atherosclerosis (a disease in which the arteries narrow and fur up), that can make it difficult to get an erection. Some drugs, such as betablockers and some types of anti-depressant, have the same effect. Long-term smokers and drinkers also tend to be prone to erection difficulties.

If you never get erections, or you do get erections but they rarely become hard, the problem is likely to be physical (see box, opposite left). If you suspect you have physical difficulties or if you are in any doubt about your problem, it is essential that you get a thorough check-up with a doctor.

However, many men who suffer from persistent erection problems are completely healthy. In such cases, the root cause of the difficulty is emotional rather than physical.

You can make an educated guess about the origin of your erection problems. If you usually have erections when you wake up in the morning, or you can get an erection when you masturbate by yourself (but not with a partner), then your problem is probably an emotional one (see box, opposite right).

IF THE CAUSE IS PHYSICAL

There are many treatments available to deal with erectile difficulties – your doctor can go through the options with you. They include the following:

- A penis pump and penis ring – you place the cylinder of the pump device around your penis and then pump the air out to create a vacuum. This draws blood into the penis making it erect. The ring goes around the base of the penis to keep the erection firm.

- Sildenafil (Viagra) is probably the most well-known drug for treating erection problems. It's available on prescription. You take it about an hour before you want to have sex and it helps you get an erection by increasing the blood supply to the penis.

- Penile injections – you inject a drug directly into the shaft of the penis and this produces an erection.

- Penile implants – these are inserted into the penis by a urologist and they can be inflated whenever you want to have an erection. Some implants leave the penis in a state of permanent semi-rigidity.

IF THE CAUSE IS EMOTIONAL

Anger, guilt, depression, boredom and self-doubt are just some of the emotions that can lead to erection problems. For example, you could be angry with your partner for having an affair, or be feeling guilty about an infidelity of your own. You might be depressed about life in general. Or perhaps you are bored with the way you and your partner make love, or are even experiencing doubts about your sexuality. Sometimes an excessive amount of self-consciousness can translate into erection problems.

Unfortunately, there's no fast or easy symptom relief for emotionally-induced erection problems. As a first step to recovery, it is vital that you figure out exactly what you're feeling and why. Only then can you attempt to resolve the underlying problem. The questions on the right may help you to address some of the important issues.

- Is it obvious why you're having erection problems? If so, can you share the reasons with your partner? Could the two of you try a self-help program, such as the sex detox described on pages 50–53? The sex detox takes away all the performance pressure of having to have erections and orgasms during sex and helps you to take a more relaxed and sensual approach.

- Is the problem likely to be a temporary one? For example, have you just started sleeping with a new partner and is your desire to impress him or her making you anxious? Would it be better to see how things progress, rather than drawing attention to what may be a transient problem?

- Do you think your erection problems are related to stress or depression? The desire to have sex often disappears completely when you're under a lot of pressure or feeling down. Would it help to learn stress-management techniques or seek treatment for depression?

- Are you confused about why you're having erection problems? Would speaking to a counsellor or sex therapist be helpful?

CONCLUSION

Whether you have completely reexamined your sex life or discovered that you are pretty much happy with things just the way they are, I hope that this book has filled you with ideas, inspiration and enthusiasm about sex. By now you will know, hopefully from first-hand experience, that sex is about much more than genital stimulation – it's a meeting of two bodies and minds that can provide some amazing physical, emotional and even spiritual feelings. You will also know that because our sex lives are underpinned by such a dense mass of emotions, attitudes, beliefs and hopes, sex can be a very complex part of human relationships. Sometimes it's necessary to go back to the basics – to talk about what we expect from our sex lives, to examine whether what we do in bed makes us happy and to look at the strength of our relationship with our partner. This book provides you with practical exercises that, I hope, have enabled you to do all of these things.

Perhaps you would like to continue your sexual voyage in some way. You might like to learn more about yoga, meditation or Tantrism so that you can become more mindful when you make love. You may have enjoyed massage so much that you want to learn more by reading a book dedicated to the subject or by going to classes. Maybe you and your partner have looked at your relationship and have decided that the most positive way forward is to seek sex therapy or counselling. Whichever direction you choose to go in, you will find plenty of leads on page 148 (Further Reading) and page 149 (Useful Addresses).

But by far the best way to augment your sexual experience is to keep having sex that is exploratory, questioning, interesting and sensual. If you find your sex life becoming predictable or old sexual problems or hang-ups keep rearing their head, return to this book, reappraise your sexual style and challenge yourself to find new ways of thinking about sex and of relating to your partner. It's worth it – through our sex lives we can experience some of the most sensual and connected feelings that life has to offer.

FURTHER READING

Barbach, Lonnie Garfield *For Each Other: Sharing Sexual Intimacy* (Anchor Books, New York, 1983)

Bishop, Clifford *Living Wisdom: Sex and Spirit* (Duncan Baird Publishers, London, 1996)

Blank, Joani *Good Vibrations: The New Complete Guide to Vibrators* (Down There Press, San Francisco, 1999)

Cox, Tracey *Hot Sex* (Corgi, London and Bantam, New York, 1999)

Fraser, Tara *Yoga for You* (UK)/ *Total Yoga* (US) (Duncan Baird Publishers, London and Thorsons, USA, 2001)

Friday, Nancy *Forbidden Flowers: Women's Sexual Fantasies* (Arrow, London, 1994 and Pocket Books, New York, 1993)

Friday, Nancy *Men In Love* (Arrow, London, 1980 and Delta, New York, 1998)

Friday, Nancy *My Secret Garden* (Quartet Books, London, 1979 and Pocket Books, New York, 1998)

Friday, Nancy *Women On Top* (Arrow, London and Pocket Books, New York, 1993)

Heiman, Julia R. and LoPiccolo, Joseph *Becoming Orgasmic* (Piatkus, London, 1988 and Fireside Books, New York, 1987)

Hite, Shere *The Hite Report* (Hamlyn, London, 2000 and Seven Stories Press, New York, 2003)

Hooper, Anne *The Body Electric* (HarperCollins, London, 1984)

Hooper, Anne *Ultimate Sex* (Dorling Kindersley, London and New York, 2001)

Litvinoff, Sarah *The Relate Guide to Sex in Loving Relationships* (Vermilion, London, 1992)

Love, Patricia and Robinson, Jo *Hot Monogamy* (Piatkus, London, 1998 and Plume, USA, 1999)

Masters, William, H. et al *Human Sexuality* (Addison-Wesley, Boston, USA, 1995)

Sampson, Val *Tantra: The Art of Mind-Blowing Sex* (Vermilion, London, 2002)

Semans, Anne and Winks, Cathy *The Good Vibrations Guide to Sex: The Most Complete Sex Manual Ever Written* (Cleis Press, San Francisco, 2002)

Smith, Karen *Massage: The Healing Power of Touch* (Duncan Baird Publishers, London, 1998 and Thorsons, USA, 2003)

Sternberg, Robert, J. *Love Is a Story: A New Theory of Relationships* (Oxford University Press, Oxford, 1998)

Tannen, Deborah *You Just Don't Understand* (Virago, London, 1992 and Quill, New York, 2001)

Winks, Cathy *The Good Vibrations Guide: The G-Spot* (Down There Press, San Francisco, 1999)

Zilbergeld, Bernie *The New Male Sexuality* (Bantam, New York, 1999)

USEFUL ADDRESSES

UK

Ann Summers
Gold Group House
Godstone Road
Whyteleafe
Surrey CR3 0GG
www.annsummers.co.uk

British Association for Sexual and Relationship Therapy (BASRT)
PO Box 13686
London SW20 9ZH
www.basrt.org.uk

The British Wheel of Yoga
25 Jermyn Street
Sleaford
Lincolnshire NG34 7RU
www.bwy.org.uk

Family Planning Association (FPA)
2–12 Pentonville Road
London N1 9FP
www.fpa.org.uk

The Impotence Association
PO Box 10296
London SW17 9WH
www.impotence.org.uk

London Lesbian and Gay Switchboard
PO Box 7324
London N1 9QS
www.llgs.org.uk

Marie Stopes International
153–157 Cleveland Street
London W1T 6QW
www.mariestopes.org.uk

Passion8
NE Services Ltd
4 Kilnbeck Business Park
Annie Reed Road
Beverley HU17 0LF
www.passion8shop.co.uk

Relate
Herbert Gray College
Little Church Street
Rugby
Warwickshire CV21 3AP
www.relate.org.uk

USA

American Massage Therapy Association
820 Davis Street
Suite 100
Evanston IL 60201-4444
www.amtamassage.org

Good Vibrations
938 Howard Street
Suite 101
San Francisco CA 94103
www.goodvibes.com

The Institute for Advanced Study of Human Sexuality
1523 Franklin Street
San Francisco CA 94109-4522
www.iashs.edu

Institute for Marital and Sexual Therapy
PO Box 210278
Chula Vista CA
210278-0278
www.sexualtherapy.com

Planned Parenthood Federation of America
810 Seventh Avenue
New York NY 10019
www.plannedparenthood.org

Society for Human Sexuality
PMB 1276
1122 East Pike Street
Seattle WA 98122-3934
www.sexuality.org

INDEX

ACKNOWLEDGMENTS

The publisher would like to thank the following people and photographic libraries for permission to reproduce their material. Every care has been taken to trace copyright holders. However, if we have omitted anyone we apologize and will, if informed, make corrections in any future edition.

Page 14 bottom right Bruce Ayres/Getty Images, London; 79 Spencer Rowell/Getty Images, London; 85 Ron Chapple/Getty Images, London; 93 International Stock/ImageState, London; 102 top David Hanover/Getty Images, London; 108 centre left Timothy Shonnard/Getty Images, London

Models for commissioned photography supplied by International Model Managagement (IMM), London

Anne Hooper would like to thank Kesta Desmond, for inspiration, verbal dexterity and plain hard work

John Davis is represented by Gina Phillips